Anyone who spends a few minutes with Andy and Joan can't help but catch something—like vision, energy, enthusiasm, and missionary zeal!

—*Joni Eareckson Tada*, Founder of Joni and Friends International Ministries

Joan and Andy Horner represent the highest levels of integrity. They have become leaders in our industry and have done it the right way.

—*Neil Offen*, President, Direct Selling Association

Andy Horner spent seventeen years at Home Interiors and he affected us. Although he moved on, that did not erase the imprint he made; it's still there and we're better off for it.

—*Donald J. Carter*, former CEO and Chairman of the Board, Home Interiors and Gifts

The launching of Premier Designs through Andy and Joan Horner was verily and truly a providence of God. In the devoted and dedicated people who work for the company, and in the many recipients of the goodness and kindness of the organization, a whole generation has been marvelously blessed.

—*W. A. Criswell*, Pastor/Pastor Emeritus, 1944–2002, First Baptist Church, Dallas, Texas

D0897390

In a world that is crying for caring, Andy and Joan heard. Their awesome creation, Premier Designs, reflects and supports the much deeper beauty of two lives dedicated to God's designs of spreading His truth in the ministry of healing—spiritually, emotionally, and physically.

—***Dr. Hazel Goddard***, Founder of Christian Counseling Ministries

If Andy and Joan were described to me without having met them, I don't think I could believe they were real people. Real? Are they ever! Real Christians. Real workers. Real examples. Their love for the Lyons family has been an immeasurable blessing. Their involvement in our Chicago inner city ministry has been an incredible encouragement. Real friends. Real servants.

—***Charles Lyons***, Pastor, Armitage Baptist Church, Chicago, Illinois

In the first century it was the couple Aquila and Priscilla who shook the world for Jesus Christ. In the twenty-first century it is Andy and Joan Horner who are turning the world upside down with the Gospel message. Their miraculous story is a reminder of what an extraordinary God can do through anyone who is sold out to serving Him and serving others.

—***Robert Jeffress,*** Senior Pastor, First Baptist Church, Dallas, Texas

By Chance or By Design?

THE STORY OF PREMIER DESIGNS & FOUNDERS, ANDY AND JOAN HORNER

ANDREW J. HORNER

WITH ANDREA HORNER, PH.D. AND DAVE WYRTZEN, TH.D.

Premier Designs
INC.

꙳

*This book is dedicated with deepest gratitude to my
sweet wife, Joan, and all who helped build Premier Designs in
this first generation. I am 86 years old now as I write this. Joan
and I have been married for 64 wonderful years, and Premier
has been in business for 25 successful years. Improbable as it
sometimes seems, this is a true story—an amazing unfolding
of God's design for my life in spite of my early rebellion against
Him. It's an amazing thing to see God's plan through all these
years of walking with Him. God blessed me more than I
deserved when He gave me Joan and an awesome family—five
children, sixteen grandchildren and three great-grandchildren—
all of whom are incredibly special. My cup runneth over with
thanks to God for what He has done! God will do the same for
you—give you purpose, hope and joy—if you invite Christ into
your life. That is my hope and prayer in writing this book, that
it will inspire you to allow God to work in you and through
you in a new and marvelous way. To God
be the glory now and forever!*

꙳

Contents

PART III: THE GROWTH OF PREMIER

PART IV: THE FUTURE OF PREMIER

PART V: THE PROOF OF PREMIER

Preface

s Premier Designs enters its twenty-fifth year, it's wise to reflect on the past and let it inform the future. Our hope in November of 1985 was to establish a company of direct service, not just direct selling. It was hard for Joan and me to define what we truly dreamed of and what we felt God desired for us and our company. We wanted a business that would be different. As we think back over all that has happened, we know without a doubt that this company was established by design.

Premier Designs is unique. It is built on a solid foundation of principles from the Bible. The Bible teaches us about the important things in life and business, such as integrity, love, how truth always prevails, that giving is more of a blessing than receiving, what true service is all about, and the way to find real joy and peace. Our Philosophy (that we believe in God who created every person with worth and value), our

Purpose (to enrich every life we touch) and our Plan (to serve through Home Shows, to go into the homes of America with a smile on our faces and hope in our hearts) all contribute to Premier's uniqueness. Because of our Biblical foundation and how we have stayed secure in it, God has truly blessed Premier.

The uniqueness of Premier Designs is also illustrated in the four original reasons we had for beginning this business:

1. We wanted to offer an opportunity for mothers to be able to stay home more with their children.
2. We wanted to encourage single parents by providing a way to increase their self-esteem and do something worthwhile while supporting their children.
3. We wanted a company that would provide a way for individuals to meet their financial needs, especially people in full-time Christian work, wives of pastors, and church staff members.
4. We wanted a company that would help support Christian ministries and charities in America and around the world.

After a year of prayer, thought and discussion, Joan and I made the tough decision—one I really didn't want to make—to start a jewelry company. You may ask, "Why didn't you want to make that decision?" Well, after spending seventeen years with a direct sales company, I was burned out. The thought of working with another direct sales company was not appealing to me. It was different for Joan. She was sad at having lost many friends when we left the former company, and so she was more ready. She has always built strong, personal relationships. So we started Premier in 1985, and that decision has changed not only our lives but also the lives of thousands of others. Little did we know twenty-five years ago that our desire to help people meet their needs would continue to be our driving force today.

Now that we are in our mid-eighties, Joan and I find ourselves wondering about the future of Premier Designs. Being such a successful and growing company, can we trust the next generation of Premier Leadership to stay true to our Founding Principles and Reasons for Existence? We have prayed a lot about the second generation of Premier. We are still very active and enjoy the opportunity to serve our Premier Family. We are very happy to share with you that we believe our second generation is in very good hands.

In 2007, after much prayer and serious discussion, our son Tim agreed to become our President. Before that, Tim worked for more than a decade developing and building Premier Manufacturing, which supplies us with a good part of our product line. We established a great working relationship during those years, and he gained a greater knowledge of what Premier Designs is all about. In these few years as our President, he has made some necessary and well-timed changes. These changes and improvements at our Home Office and Distribution Center have increased our production and our ability to serve the Premier Family. We are having some of the best years ever! This is great, but there is something much more important. Tim is wholeheartedly committed to continuing Premier Designs just as it was founded. He believes in our Philosophy, Purpose and Plan, in our Reasons for Existence, and in our Biblical Foundation. He's very honest and is a hard worker. His belief in good management and maintaining a financially strong, debt-free company gives us great confidence that what has made Premier successful in the past will continue under his direction.

In addition, we have a wonderful Home Management Team who serve our Premier Family, and an incredible Field Leadership Team, along with our wonderful Jewelers, who will continue to serve in the homes of America. We appreciate them so much. They have each contributed to the success of Premier and will help make our future strong.

We pray that God will continue to bless Premier, and that our Founding Verse will continue to be our objective: "The Lord demands fairness in every business deal. He established this principle" (Proverbs 16:11, TLB). Premier belongs to the Direct Selling Association (DSA), a solid national association that does much for the direct sales industry. They operate with integrity, which is very important to us. Their Code of Ethics must be adopted and followed closely by each company. We are a proud member of the DSA and appreciate all they do to safeguard our industry. May we continue serving others with fairness and integrity. Let's always be looking to our future, where we will have more opportunities to serve, share and care.

Premier's Biblical Foundation and Principles have not changed, but new technology is flourishing. In this regard, Premier will always do WIR-WBP (What Is Right—What Is Best for Premier). May we never forget the secrets of our success and endeavor to always keep a personal touch. People need to know they are special and unique.

Joan and I believe wholeheartedly that Premier is a miracle. My wife of sixty-four years, Joan has been a part of everything from the beginning. She is a wonderful balance for me. Her great desire is to "Keep It Personal," an underlying philosophy that has truly contributed to our success. Another of her contributions is to select the Scripture Verse of the Year, which is presented every January at our nationwide conferences. For 2010 she selected Psalm 115:1, "Not to us, O LORD, but to you goes all the glory for your unfailing love and faithfulness" (NLT). This verse clearly sums up our thoughts about the success of Premier Designs throughout these twenty-five years. God is the faithful One who has blessed our efforts. All the glory goes to Him.

Andy Horner, CSO
July 2010

Acknowledgments

Many of the ideas in this book are not original, but have come from those who have had a great impact on my life. I thank all who have shared with me and taught me, especially:

My mother, *Sarah Smyth Horner*, an Irish scrub lady who gave birth to sixteen children, who had no education but was so wise. She instilled in me the qualities of hard work and persistence. She prayed for me, disciplined me, loved me and always demanded my best.

Lorne Lynch, owner of Lynch's Meat Market, who taught me when I was a young lad the value of hard work; *Jay Lansford*, my first manager at Johnson Wax, who was hard to please but taught me much; *Dr. William Smith*, of Xerox, who convinced me that I had strengths, but also weaknesses; and *Mary Crowley*, founder of Home Interiors, who taught me so much, but nothing more important than, "You build the people and they will build your business." She reminded me that you cannot outgive God and taught me not to look at people as they appear, but to see in them what they can become. A woman of true integrity, she practiced what she preached.

How can I express my gratitude to *Joan*, my wife of over sixty years? Her encouragement, love, patience and help have changed my life. Her desire to do what is right and in the right way keeps me on the right track. It is true that behind every successful man is a dedicated, supportive woman. To my five grown children, *Andrea*, *Sarah*, *Tim*, *Mary* and *Tommy*, all gifts from God, who had to eat and so kept me motivated. When I might have quit, they were the reason I did not.

Special thanks to *Andrea Horner*, my daughter, who researched and wrote most of this story, and *Dave Wyrtzen*, my counselor and friend, who helped Andrea try to fit eighty years into these pages. They know me well and have presented the story as it was and is. For this Fourth Edition, I want to extend my thanks to my granddaughter *Kathryn* and my daughter *Mary Horner Collins*, who helped update and edit this new edition.

My prayer is that this book may honor the Lord whom I serve and be a blessing to those who are kind enough to read its pages.

Introduction

*S*uccess in the Internet generation is about mastering new technology. Computerized telephone answering services, voice mail, faxes, spread sheets, cell phones and e-mail—these are the tools needed to achieve a prosperous bottom line in the communication age.

My name is Michael. As a graduate of a prestigious university with a degree in business, I thought I knew what it takes to build a successful company in a technological world. Then my wife, Linda, met a friend who was involved in selling jewelry. They met for lunch, and Linda noticed the exquisite earrings that set off her friend's stylish outfit. "Mary, where did you get those earrings, and where did you get the money to dress like that?" she asked.

Mary laughed. "They're not all that expensive and if you'll come to Barbara's house tomorrow night, I'll show you a lot more than these earrings."

Linda went to the show and did come home with a lot more than jewelry. "Michael, look at what I bought!"

She modeled her evening purchases—Runway necklace, Knockout bracelet and Companion earrings. Even the names sounded rich and exotic, and I responded with the required oohs and ahs. Then she dropped the bomb. "Michael, this is terrific stuff and we can sell it!"

Sell it? The last thing I wanted was for my wife to get involved in some direct sales jewelry company. But Linda continued, "I want to start my own business like Mary. This Premier Designs company offers an incredible opportunity. Look at this marketing plan."

Just what I needed—my wife involved in some get-rich-quick, multilevel pyramid scheme. But I did look at the plan, and instead of high-sounding promises, there was the authentic ring of down-home values, good old American hard work, and basic common sense. When Linda made over four hundred dollars at her first Home Show, it seemed it wouldn't hurt for her to go ahead. She would soon burn out, and it would be time for her to try to find herself in some other crazy dream.

Rather than burning out, however, she became more excited, her confidence soared, and her business grew steadily. I found myself caring for our kids a couple of nights a week, especially as Linda's Home Show schedule accelerated before the Christmas holidays. After New Year's, things would settle down and our home could return to normal, I thought. Or would it?

"Michael, I've won an achievement award!" Linda told me excitedly. "I want you to come to the Rally with me. It will be good for us. We can meet new friends. I can get new ideas for developing my business, and you can evaluate Premier Designs for yourself." So we sent in our registrations, and I found myself checking into the Dallas hotel.

How do you describe a Premier Designs Rally? It's a combination of business-training seminar, old-fashioned revival and camp meeting, pep rally, and warm family reunion. It's a cross between a Billy Graham crusade and a *Jeopardy* show. Linda and I found ourselves deep in the heart of Texas hustling from seminars on "Managing Your Money" to training sessions covering bookings, Home Shows, and managing your time and your business. I've never hugged so many people, seen so many smiles and felt such honest concern.

There was no hype about how you could be driving a brand-new Cadillac and vacationing in Cancun if you simply signed on. Instead, I heard testimonies of single mothers who found friends, a support system, and a way to meet their financial needs and be with their kids. Former contractors and engineers shared how they survived seismic shifts in their industry, paid off their debts, and found fulfillment by building into the lives of others when they found Premier. These people talked not about "direct sales" but about "direct service." They talked about "enriching every life they touched," "remembering that people are more important than profits," and that "every individual is worthy and valuable, not because of what they do, but because God created them in His own image."

Was all this too good to be true? Could these traditional values of honesty, caring and giving provide a foundation for a company that would be successful in the twenty-first century? Modern companies talk about aggressive attack, hostile takeovers and warlike competition. How could there be room in American business for a company that functions more like a nostalgic rerun of *The Waltons* than the latest *Die Hard* movie? A company that has integrity and tells the truth? A company that emphasizes that building a successful life is more important than building a successful business?

The growth of Premier Designs provided the objective proof I needed. Who could argue with the numbers? Premier is successful—through solid Home Office management, controlled growth in sales, skilled personnel, exquisite products and careful planning for the future. The most hardened cynic could not argue with this.

But statistics do not answer deeper issues of credibility and trust. I received my answer to these questions on the Saturday morning of the Rally as Andy Horner, the Founder of Premier, shared from his heart.

As the orchestra and chorus came to the crescendo of their "Tribute to America," patriotism moistened everyone's eyes. Andy's heart for his adopted homeland was evident as he spoke. Where else on earth could the son of an alcoholic father, born into the hate and violence of Belfast, end up the cofounder and president of a successful company dedicated to honoring God and serving others? A stool was set center stage and Andy casually sat down. It was time to deliver his annual founder's address, entitled "Lest We Forget." He told more than the story of his life; he told the story of Premier Designs.

This company and the truths it demonstrates have changed my life. It could change yours. It has given me renewed hope. Yes, this former no-nonsense business

cynic with his spread sheets and fax machines has recognized the revolutionary power of personal serving, caring
and giving even in the jungle of American business. It is
no longer Linda's business; it is our business. The following pages explain why.

PART ONE

The Road

to

Premier

*"Adventures always have risks, but
they also have rewards. Don't let
the past, good or bad, affect your present
or determine your future."*

ANDY HORNER

*"The things about my mother that I
resented as a boy are the things that
I am most grateful for as a man."*

ANDY HORNER

CHAPTER ONE

Irish Roots

Joan and I incorporated Premier Designs in Dallas, Texas, in November 1985, but the beginnings of Premier can really be traced all the way back to Ireland in the 1920s. It's been a long road with many hills and valleys. Has it been easy? No. And for most of my years I was unaware of my final destination.

LAST IN LINE

I was born at 3 Upper Charleville Street in Belfast on August 5, 1924, to Sarah Smyth and Andrew Horner. My mother worked in the linen factories as a weaver before her marriage, and part-time even after she had children. My father worked his entire life as a welder at the famous Belfast shipyards. Six days a week, he left for work in the dark each morning and came home after dark each night.

It was a difficult life. We had enough to eat, but barely, and wore hand-me-down clothes a size too big. There were enough coins to buy gas for the light and peat for the fire, but nothing extra. I can remember being excited to get an orange and some candy in my Christmas stocking.

I am sure that by 1924 my mother thought she was done having babies. The youngest of her twelve surviving children was seven years old. The tiny Irish row house had only a small living room and kitchen downstairs and two small bedrooms upstairs. The children slept four or five to a straw mattress and ate meals sitting on the stairs. When one of the kids left home, it was a big deal—it meant the next oldest got to graduate to the table. The household was already overflowing. Nonetheless, at age forty-four, my mother learned she was pregnant once again—with me.

I was born at home, delivered by my mother's sister. She and my mother were the neighborhood midwives. My brothers and sisters didn't exactly welcome me with open arms. I was one more mouth to feed and one more child to take care of. My mother said that I was her "angel pride from heaven sent," but the rest of the family thought I had been sent from somewhere else—and most of the time, it felt like they wanted to send me back there.

Looking back on it, I can understand their feelings. Not only were we poor and living in a crowded house, but I cried constantly. Later we found out that I had been crying because of chronic ear infections and an abscessed eardrum. But at the time, all the other children knew was that there was this fussy baby who made their lives even more difficult. As I grew older, their feeling that I was an afterthought and a bother remained the same. They did not hide the fact that they would rather not have me around. My mother made them play with me, and if they didn't, I told on them. Of course they considered me a tattletale pest and a tag-along. Whenever they could, they left me behind. If we played hide-and-seek, I would hide but they never came to find me. Even when I was older and we played cowboys and Indians, they would make me be the Indian, tie me to a tree and leave me there. One day my brother Hughey got so disgusted with me that he threw me in a lake. I quickly learned how to swim!

Now I tell these stories as jokes, but they had an impact on me. I carried the feelings of rejection and being unwanted for many, many years—feelings forced even deeper inside by the pressure of growing up in a religiously divided country where I was taught to hate and fight. Only later in life did I learn that feelings can deceive us.

BELFAST BATTLES

Ireland, an island the size of the state of Maine, is perched in the beautiful North Atlantic, surrounded by 1,700 miles of dramatic coastline. The Irish are friendly and hospitable, and among the most creative people on this earth. Ireland has produced more poets, playwrights and American Presidents than any other country of comparable size.

There is another side to Ireland, though. It is a place filled with hatred, bigotry and violence. The people are proud and strong-willed. As a Protestant,

I was brought up to hate and fear Catholics. Groups of Catholic toughs would cross the Crumlin Road—the division between the Protestant and Catholic neighborhoods—and harass us. They threw rocks and bottles, broke up our games, stole our balls, and taunted us. These battles weren't one-sided; we did our share of rock throwing as well. We felt vulnerable and learned at tender ages about hatred and intimidation.

In those days, the battles of my world carried over into our home. My dad was not around much. When he was, he had little to say. On payday, he joined his buddies at the pub and got drunk. When he got drunk, he got mean—almost every weekend was hell. I remember him roaring into our house many Saturday nights yelling, busting down doors, looking for a fight. Only my big brother Bill could control him. He would take Dad out of the house and walk him around until he sobered up. It was a hopeless life, both inside and outside our home, and when Bill emigrated to America in 1929, it got worse. Now there was no one to protect us from Catholic bullies and a drunken father.

Things became very desperate for our family. My mother loved Ireland and Charleville Street, her friends and family. But she wanted better for her children. Unbeknownst to my father, she made the biggest decision of her life—she decided to take me, my brother Hugh and my sister Chrissie away from Ireland. Four of my brothers had already gone. Bill and Tommy were in America, and Sammy and Jim were in Canada. She wanted to take us to America, but health problems prevented this; so my brothers arranged for our passage to Canada.

THE DUCHESS OF RICHMOND

I still vividly remember the morning of April 8, 1931. A big, black car drove up in front of our house to drive us to the dock. I had never even seen a car before, let alone ridden in one, and I was excited. I raced around trying to hurry everyone up, running back and forth looking into the car. Finally, we all got in and drove off. I could hardly sit still. I squirmed from window to window trying to make sure that I didn't miss a thing. And then there she was, sitting in the Belfast harbor—the *Duchess of Richmond*, the big, beautiful ship that was going to take us to Canada. I didn't understand much about what we were doing or where we were going, but I was excited. I can remember walking on board and seeing the huge crystal chandeliers and the long tables loaded with food. I had never seen anything like this before, and certainly had never seen so much food. I couldn't wait for us to get going so I could start eating.

A group of friends from the Gospel Hall came to see us off. My mother had become a Christian before I was born, and she was a faithful member of the Machette Street Gospel Hall. Those Christian folks gathering around us to pray and sing just before we left is one of the sweetest memories I have of my childhood in Ireland. I can still hear them:

> *God be with you till we meet again;*
> *By His counsels guide, uphold you,*
> *With His sheep securely fold you;*
> *God be with you till we meet again.*

And then we were off. It was an act of faith, courage and sacrifice for my fifty-one-year-old mother to leave her husband, family, friends and beloved Ireland to give her youngest children opportunity and hope. Little did she know that the journey she began that day would lead, fifty-four years later, to the adventure of Premier Designs, a company that would touch thousands of lives in America and around the world with opportunity and hope. Was it the luck of the Irish? Just by chance? Or was there a greater design?

"The legacy my mother left was not silver
or gold, but was worth so much more.
She taught me how to work hard and that it
was more blessed to give than to receive."

ANDY HORNER

"If a thing is worth doing,
it is worth doing well."

SARAH HORNER, Andy's mother

"A sense of worth is not found in titles, in
possessions, or in who we know; but is found
in our relationship with God."

ANDY HORNER

CHAPTER TWO

Woodstock Memories

After two weeks at sea, our ship arrived in St. John's, New Brunswick, and we boarded a train to Woodstock. It was a journey of over a thousand miles. All we had to eat was a can of cookies given as a going-away gift. When we arrived in the city of Woodstock, Ontario, there was no one there to meet us. I never did discover what caused the mix-up, but there we were, four Irish immigrants, standing on the train platform in a strange town in Canada. My mother did not wait long. There were only two cabs in town. She hailed one of them and asked the driver if he knew where Sam Horner lived. Surprisingly, he did. He drove us straight to 715 Dundas Street, above the Maple Dairy store. We climbed up eight flights of stairs and walked inside the flat where I was to live for the next fifteen years.

THE WOODSTOCK PAPERBOY

Compared to the fragments I remember of Ireland, my memories of Canada are full and vivid. The thing I remember most is work, work, work. At age seven, I started tossing papers. No matter what other activities or jobs I had going, I met the 5:30 p.m. train from Toronto, rain or snow, six afternoons a week, to get my papers to deliver. At the age of nine, I began working Saturdays at Lynch's Meat Market earning seventy-five cents a day; and at eleven, working summers and after school at the Maple Dairy, washing milk bottles, wrapping butter and delivering orders. I sold produce (carrots and beans) door-to-door for five cents a bunch. I helped my mother scrub the floors and stairs in our building in exchange for free rent and ice. There were 120 steps and I remember every one. I calculated that I did this detested chore 520 times! We also cleaned apartments and offices night after night. Through it all, I kept throwing those newspapers.

Mother was from the old country culture that believed in hard work and no complaining. And my work never ended. Over and over again she made me do a job until I got it right. Talk about a hard taskmaster and a tough disciplinarian! I felt persecuted and picked on. She maintained strict standards and she expected me to meet them all. At the time I felt she was unfair and constantly punishing me, and I resented it. Now I cherish those values and work habits that she pounded into me. I can still hear her saying, "A job worth doing is worth doing right" and "Work as unto the Lord." Because of her legacy, I've never been afraid to work hard, and I never leave a job half done.

I also learned that "a penny saved is a penny earned." The poverty of Ireland and the hardships in Canada during the 1930s depression made frugality an absolute necessity for our family. Once, after I had collected the money for my paper route, I dropped a dime in the snow on my way home. Mom made me go all the way back to where I had dropped it and dig around in the snow until I found it. Cold, humiliated, ashamed, I resented her making me scrounge around in the snow for one measly dime; but slowly I was learning the value of even one thin coin.

We ate day-old bread and cracked eggs. In fact, I thought all eggs came cracked. We never used more electricity or gas than absolutely necessary. We had to turn the lights off in every room as we left (a habit that continues to this day). At night we sat in the dark to cut down the light bill. Mother had few dresses, and we wore hand-me-downs that didn't fit. I had to tighten my belt to hold up pants that were too large. Mom made my pant cuffs inches deep so she could let them out as I grew. I hated being poor and felt embarrassed wearing those too-large castoffs, but I can still hear my mother say, "Son, you'll grow into them. It's what's on the inside that counts."

Liberal generosity is hardly expected from someone who works constantly just to pay the light bill, but my mother was one of the most generous people I ever knew. If you walked into her house and said you liked something, it was on your doorstep the next morning. People learned to be careful what they said about stuff in our house because it was easy to end up with something you didn't really like or want. Many times she gave away our food, clothing and furniture. We would go without so someone else could have something they needed.

My mother's Bible is a precious treasure to me. It is in the Bible collection at Premier's Home Office, and whenever I look through it, one thing always strikes me—it is filled with prayer cards and pledge cards for a number of missionaries. She told me that there was no greater thing we could do than help spread the Gospel to all the world, and although she did not have much money, she gave generously. Her heart was with missions.

Mother gave more than her money, however; she gave herself. When she died in May of 1947, her funeral was one of the largest the city of Woodstock had ever seen. I was shocked. Hundreds of people came to pay their respects to this Irish scrub lady. We heard story after story of her many kindnesses. People I had never met told me how she had given them a gift of bread or soup, had nursed them and cared for their children, and had always had kind words of comfort, encouragement and love. She left me a marvelous legacy of hard work and selfless giving.

THE WOODSTOCK LETTERMAN

Yes, I worked hard, but that's not all I did as a boy. I entered the Chapel School at seven, the Princess School at ten, and the Woodstock Collegiate High School at thirteen. I was not what you would call a great student. Although I never failed a grade, I remained firmly planted near the bottom of my class. I preferred the social life. Visiting with my friends was a much higher priority than doing common, everyday homework. I was very talkative, liked being the center of attention, and couldn't sit still. I also had a short attention span and had difficulty focusing on one thing at a time. I tell people that I spent more time in the principal's office than in my classroom, which may be an Irishman's slight exaggeration, but not by much. Even though my mother's favorite expression was "Children are to be seen and not heard," I was heard every time I was seen.

Because of my short attention span and my hands that sometimes shook, schools tested me regularly to figure out what was wrong with me. They tried pills to calm me down and help me concentrate, but nothing worked. I guess today they would diagnose me as hyperactive with attention deficit disorder, but back then they didn't have scientific labels for such things. They simply called me a pain in the neck.

Combine bad grades, bad behavior and bad placement at the end of the line in a large family, and you've got the ingredients for some low self-esteem. And then there were sports. I was a short, scrawny kid, too small to really be competitive, but I loved playing and had a strong desire to win. I had something to prove.

We had some athletic talent in my family. Bill, my older brother, played championship soccer in Ireland and professional soccer in the States. Despite the athletic genes passed down to the Horners, I had to overcome my size disadvantage by doing what I knew best—working at it harder than anyone else. I went to the YMCA and shot baskets hour after hour. Every spare minute, I was on the ice fine-tuning my hockey skills. I played catch and batted baseballs with anyone who would play with me. As a result, I played hockey and basketball all through high school, starring and lettering in both. In the summers I was one of the stars of city league baseball. My lack of achievement in the classroom is now legendary, and my musical career peaked when I performed my one instrumental solo, "Nearer My God to Thee," on my one-dollar guitar. But athletics was the one place where my strong drive could generate success and I could get the recognition I craved. I had to be the best and I had to win. Sports became the way to do this, because I sure wasn't that great in much else.

Sometimes I took this striving to achieve and needing to win too far. At one race at a school event, when I saw that I was not going to win, I simply pulled up and acted like I was hurt and unable to finish the race. If you can't win, I figured, then fake an injury. This approach also brought the added advantage of getting all that attention over my "injured leg."

WOODSTOCK'S "MR. PERSONALITY"

As I look back, one thing that was evident during my growing-up years in Woodstock was my ability to relate to people. Whatever other struggles I had inside myself and in my life, I always liked people and could get along well with them. One example stands out in my mind. Thanks to the generosity of Jack Cole, one of our town's leaders, every summer I was able to go to Fisher's Glen, a YMCA camp. Two summers in a row I was elected "Best All Around Boy." This was quite an honor, and I was one of the few boys who received it more than once. Natural leadership abilities were beginning to show up in my life—enthusiasm, a knack for understanding people, an outgoing personality, and an ability to get along with just about anyone. These traits have helped me overcome a lot and became important in my business success. I am grateful for the early opportunities through athletics and summer camp to develop these leadership characteristics.

Friends, awards at camp, and success in athletics were all a part of my childhood—but my dad wasn't. I never saw or heard from him after we left Ireland, and my memories of him are not positive. I saw other kids with their dads and imagined what it would be like to have a nice dad. I would go to the homes of my friends like Bob and Jimmy Davis and pretend that their families, especially their fathers, were mine. Their mom made us delicious donuts, and their dad wrestled with us and helped us build things. I remember other dads who played ball with their sons and me, and who took me places and did things with me. These men were kind and took an interest in me, but it wasn't the same as having a father of my own. A dad, a nice home, and a normal family life—that's what I longed for.

THE WOODSTOCK DECISION

When we arrived in Woodstock, one of the first things my mother did was go to the nearby Gospel Hall to apply for membership. However, the Woodstock Brethren would not allow her to join their congregation because she didn't have the proper letter from her Brethren congregation in Ireland. They made us sit in the visitors' section at the back of the hall. With this reception, it didn't take us long to end up down the street at Oxford Street Baptist Church, a small congregation of one hundred people that became the center of our lives.

I know my mother's faith took on even deeper

meaning for her in Canada than it had in Ireland. She missed Ireland and her friends and family. She was lonely and heartbroken, and I heard her crying many nights as she sat rocking in the dark. She sacrificed a great deal to bring us to Canada. Mom had a hard life. She was in poor health when we arrived in Woodstock, and as the years went by, her health deteriorated further. She developed a serious problem with painful and debilitating varicose veins. She suffered every day but found hope and solace in the promises of the Bible. Her relationship with the Lord sustained her and gave her a peace and joy that can't be explained. "It is no vain thing to wait upon the Lord, son," she would say.

I am ashamed to admit it, but sometimes I thought she was nuts. I would come home and hear her talking in the kitchen and think we had company, only to go back there and see that she was talking to Jesus as if He were right there in the room. She read her Bible daily and claimed its promises with unquestioning faith. I saw her kneeling by her bed countless times and heard her singing as she worked. She sang hymns of heaven and of hope—hope that her suffering would end and that soon she would be in heaven with her Lord.

For years, my mother prayed that I, too, would become a Christian. When I was eleven, her prayers were answered. I accepted Jesus Christ as my Lord and Savior at a meeting at our little Baptist church. At around the same time, my brother Hugh became a Christian at an evangelistic tent meeting in Woodstock. Hugh felt called to be an evangelist, and I went with him as he preached on the street corners of Woodstock and nearby London. He also organized a "tract band" in

Woodstock, and I helped him pass out Gospel tracts all around the city. My mother was pleased that we were both working to bring others to the Lord. For her, there was nothing more important and worthwhile.

Our lives revolved around our church. For years, we walked the mile and a half to church almost every evening. We had young people's meetings on Monday, booster band on Tuesday, prayer meeting on Wednesday, choir practice on Thursday, church socials on Friday, prayer meeting on Saturday, and three services on Sunday. My mother seldom missed, and she made me go with her. But the older I got, the less I liked it. I got tired of going to church all the time. I had other things to do that I thought were more fun. I was getting fed up with her Bible reading and praying and hymn singing, and I was sick of her telling me what I could and couldn't do.

I rebelled. I ran away a couple of times, one time hitchhiking almost twenty miles before I turned around and went back. I didn't go to church as much and started doing more things with friends who were not Christians. This worried and hurt my mother. I danced and played cards, things that my mother had taught me were sin. I stayed out late with my friends and tried to sneak in the house, and there she would be, sitting in the dark waiting for me. She disciplined me with the silent treatment. For days after one of these incidents she wouldn't speak to me, and I hated that too. I felt she wanted to control me and ruin my life.

THE WOODSTOCK PRINCESS

When I was sixteen, we got a car, a 1934 Ford. Mother

could no longer walk to our cleaning jobs, so she had to get a car in order to keep on working. I don't know where she got the money or what kind of deal she worked out for it, but she bought it. She wouldn't drive, so all the chauffeuring to and from jobs was left up to me. In the off hours, I got the car to myself.

All of a sudden I was the most popular guy in Woodstock. No one else my age had a car. Here I was, this poor kid from the East End, now running around with the rich kids from across the tracks. Although I had known these kids most of my life, we hadn't ever traveled in the same social circles. The town was socially segregated. The "East Enders" had the reputation of being poor, tough and ready to fight. Our reputation was greatly exaggerated, but we played the role well. My gang was not known for our kindness and goodness, but we were known well by the Woodstock police. I became well acquainted with Chief Innis and the other six officers.

One of the well-to-do kids from the other side of town was Joan Taylor. Joan and I had both attended elementary school at the Princess School. I used to tease her a lot when we were growing up, and through our years of schooling she had no interest in me. She was smart and always ranked first or second in class. I ranked fortieth or forty-first, depending on whether my friend George was in class that day. I tried to cheat off her a few times, too, but she wouldn't let me. She was a good, moral girl who attended church regularly. She was also the prettiest girl in Woodstock, and way out of my league.

At the time I got my car and was expanding my

social circles, Joan was dating a friend of mine named Bill. I asked out Joan's good friend, Shirley, so we could double-date. I liked Shirley, and the four of us had some great times, but I also had another agenda. I was actually courting Joan, even though she didn't know it!

Joan and I got to know each other on these outings and became good friends. I loved it when she came and cheered me on at basketball games and baseball games even when my team, the East Enders, was playing Bill's team from St. Mary's. I thought she was just super, even though she rooted for him, too. Of course, I was not going to move in on my friend, Bill, so I was just waiting for my opportunity to ask her out. Then came World War II.

When war broke out in Europe in 1939, three of my brothers joined the army and headed to England with the first Canadian division. Within the next couple of years, most of the able-bodied men in Woodstock enlisted to go fight the Germans. I was tired of school and tired of my mom and her expectations. I wanted to get away and have some adventure. So in 1941, at the age of seventeen, I joined the Royal Canadian Navy with the hope of seeing the world.

"We can't control our past;
but it's the choices we make in the present,
not what happened in the past, that will
determine our success in the future."

ANDY HORNER

"It is sad, but true, that we sometimes
do not understand, nor appreciate fully,
the impact people have until they are dead."

ANDY HORNER

CHAPTER THREE

The Navy and Romance

Over the years I've told a lot of Navy stories. For example, the first time I went on board ship, I knew something was wrong when the command came to drop anchor, and when we did, the anchor sank straight to the bottom. There was no chain connecting it to the ship. I've often described myself as the Canadian Navy's number one torpedo chaser. We had only two torpedoes, so when we fired one and missed, I had to swim out to retrieve it so we could use it again. We sank a lot of ships—the problem was that most of them were our own. We were so lethal against ourselves that the Germans planned to commission us in their Navy. I've had some fun making up jokes about my Navy days, but in fact, those were deadly serious times.

THE WAR IN THE NORTH SEA

I went to signalman's school in Quebec for several months before I ever set foot on a ship. My first ship assignment was to an ammunitions barge on the run from Montreal to St. John's, Newfoundland, down the St. Lawrence River. This was disappointing because I had visions of being assigned to a sleek fighting destroyer. Finally, I was assigned to a convoy and sailed for the North Atlantic. My ship, the *Monnow*, was a frigate and our job was to sweep ahead for German U-boats. I was so nervous I couldn't even translate the first message that came in on my watch.

After this tour, we were reassigned to a British striking force. This involved trips through the Mediterranean, and later, a six-month tour on the "hell run" from Scotland, under the Arctic Circle, to the northern Russian port of Archangel. The Germans had conquered Norway by that time and were operating both U-boats and torpedo bombers in this corridor. The run lasted twenty-six days with unbearably long nights. Our ships were coated in ice. We were in total radio silence, with the Germans below us and above us—we were sitting ducks. All communication was by lights and flags, which kept Signalman Horner V58205 very busy.

These runs were pure hell. I watched ships sinking, water flaming, and bodies of the dead floating in the seas. I was scared, and every time our ship saw action, I rededicated my life to God and asked Him to protect me. Then, as soon as the threat was gone and we got into a safe port, I went right back to acting like He didn't exist and lived it up with the rest of the guys. I was sick and tired of all the God stuff from my upbringing, and I didn't want to think about it. But I also knew something was wrong. At night in my hammock I often tossed and turned uneasily. During my entire Navy experience I never had peace.

God's faithfulness amazes me. At that point in my life I ignored Him, denied Him and ran from Him, but He never left me. He saw my three brothers and me safely through those years, while many of my friends died. Every time I go back to Woodstock, I walk through my high school and look at the pictures on the walls of my friends and schoolmates who gave their lives for our freedom. It makes me sad, but proud, when I am reminded of the sacrifices that so many made for freedom.

Woodstock was never the same after the war. So many never came home—why them and not us? Was it my mother's prayers?

ROMANCE IN WOODSTOCK

The war in Europe ended in May 1945, and I volunteered for duty in the Pacific. All who were heading for the Pacific were given a thirty-day furlough before we left. I went home for the month.

Just after arriving in Woodstock, I was downtown doing a little shopping, and Joan and a friend walked by. We talked, and she invited me to a party that night at her house. Of course I went, and we had a great time. In fact, we had such a good time that we had a date every night of my thirty-day leave! That was the big band era—a time for dances, parties and concerts in the park; a time for falling in love.

While I was busy romancing Joan, America dropped the bomb on Japan and the war in the Pacific was over. I reported back at the end of my leave and was soon discharged. I returned to Woodstock and my jobs: an order expeditor at LaFrance Textiles during the week and a meat cutter at Lynch's Meat Market on Saturdays. Joan had escaped a bad home situation by taking a job in London about thirty miles from Woodstock. Every night when I got off work, I caught the train to London to go and see her. I always tried to make the last train back to Woodstock, but usually missed it and ended up hitchhiking home after midnight. I didn't care. I was in love.

MARRIED IN WOODSTOCK

In October, Joan came to Woodstock for a weekend visit and we got engaged. We were so excited. I gave her an engagement ring, and she went home to tell her parents. Her parents ate dinner at six o'clock sharp every night, and Joan barely made it into her chair on time. Then, just as they began passing the food, she put out her left hand and said to her mom and dad, "Look what I just got." Instead of joining in her excitement, her father rapped her on the knuckles with a knife handle, as he had done many times before, and said, "There's to be no talking at this dinner table!" His cruelty hurt far more than his daughter's knuckles.

We set a June wedding date, but Joan's family remained adamantly against the marriage. Her father spoke to me bluntly, telling me this did not have his approval and asking me how on earth I thought I was going to support her on the seven dollars a week I was making. He even came to our house and tried to convince my mother to pressure me into calling it off. For

Joan's parents, this was a matter of status and appearances. They didn't want their daughter marrying the son of an Irish scrub woman from the other side of the tracks. They thought Joan could do much better than that.

My own mother could have had a stronger reason to oppose our marriage. Joan was not a Christian, and my mother wanted me to marry a Christian girl. I think we broke her heart, but she never did anything to interfere and always treated Joan very well. I wish she could have lived long enough to see Joan come to the Lord, but my mother died just a year after my marriage, a month before she was to return to Ireland. With all her children grown and out of the nest, she had made plans to go home. Instead, she went to her real home in heaven.

Family opposition aside, there was one practical obstacle to our marriage—housing was impossible to find in Woodstock. It was just after the war, and apartments were scarce. LaFrance Textiles did own an apartment building, and by a miracle, one of their tenants was moving out in February. I asked Mr. Knechtel for the apartment, and he gave it to me. Joan and I decided that there wasn't much sense in paying rent and not living in the apartment, so we moved our wedding date up three months to March 9.

Our wedding was small, but just right with close friends and family. Joan's parents did not help her in any way with the wedding, but they did come. After the ceremony, we took the train to Paris, Ontario, for a nice dinner with our entire wedding party. Then Joan and I went on to Hamilton for our one-night honeymoon. On Monday I was back at work. A year later, we made it to Niagara Falls for a real honeymoon.

Joan got a secretarial job at Ralston Purina in Woodstock, and we had fun setting up our little apartment, beginning our life together. I did have a few adjustments to make, however. One night I laid my shoes out, and Joan asked me what I was doing. I said, "Well, aren't you going to polish them?" She answered, "Polish them?" I told her that my mother always polished my shoes, and she quickly reminded me that she wasn't my mother, thus initiating our first fight. In the morning my shoes remained where I had left them, unpolished. I also left my pants lying on the floor, expecting Joan to pick them up and iron them for me just like my mother did. Soon I had to pick them up because I had only two pairs and I had to wear something to work. I learned fast that there was a major difference between a wife and a mother.

Despite these minor adjustments, we stayed in love and had a good time. We had many friends, young couples like ourselves, and had an active social life. I played basketball for the YMCA men's league. Joan and the other wives followed us all over Ontario as we played in tournaments. I got involved in the Y's service organization, and Joan joined the women's association. There were Joan's bingo parties and my beer-drinking poker parties. We raced to hockey games in the winter and baseball games in the summer. We went dancing, played cards and partied, sometimes all night long. We were on the run, and deep inside I knew that what I was really running from was the Lord.

Every once in a while I got this pang of guilt about how I was living. I even talked to Joan about her need to "get saved." I thought that if she became a Christian everything would be easier for me, but she could never understand what I was talking about. Joan was as religious as you could get. She was a moral, church-going woman, and all I could do was talk to her about her need to be "saved." "Saved from what? I can swim," she would say. "I'm not drowning!"

Within a year of our marriage we were able to buy our first house. I had picked up a third job as a ticket taker at the Green Grotto Dance Hall on Thursday nights to earn some extra money for the house. By then, Joan was not working. She had quit her job when her boss would not let her bring a radio to work to listen to the World Series! But it was just as well. She spent her time making our new house into a home. We were so excited and proud, and we loved our little house and our new neighbors. Then, in 1948, our first child, Andrea, was born. Ever since I was a boy, I had dreamed of having a home and a family, and now my dream was coming true.

It wasn't long after Andrea was born that Joan began talking seriously about moving to the States. For years she had dreamed of living there and had talked about it ever since I had known her. I couldn't really understand her strong desire. I loved Woodstock. Compared to Ireland, it seemed like heaven to me. I had planned to live out my life there. But over the months, Joan's desire to move to America became an intense passion.

THE AMERICAN DREAM

Lee Forbes, a Canadian friend who had lived in Texas for many years, was Joan's United States connection. Lee and her husband had moved to Austin, Texas, struck it rich in the oil business, and purchased a number of hotels. After her husband died, Lee returned to Woodstock and lived with Joan's aunt and uncle next door to Joan's house. Lee was blind from glaucoma, so Joan went by each afternoon to read her mail to her and write letters. Through these letters Joan got to know a number of people in Austin. Even after Lee's death, Joan continued her correspondence with these people and wanted to go and meet them. But in the late 1940s it was not easy to get to the States.

The first step in emigrating was to find a sponsor. We asked my brother Bill, who was living in the Boston area, if he would give me a job and sponsor us. He agreed. The next step was to get a visa. Joan applied under the Canadian emigration quota, and I under the Irish. There were long waiting lists for both. It took us a year to get our visas, but they finally arrived on March 17, 1950, St. Patrick's Day. We partied all night with our friends to celebrate.

Within two weeks, we had sold our house and all of our furniture and were on the train to America. We had two thousand dollars in our pockets and thought we were rich. We crossed into America at Buffalo, New York, and continued on to my brother's home, where I began working at his mill. However, within just a few weeks, it was obvious that there were some problems. Things weren't working out the way we had planned. Deciding that this would be a good time to go to Texas to visit Joan's friends, we bought ourselves a 1947 Nash, put our cedar chest, mirror and two year old in the back seat, and took off.

On the way we stopped by Washington, D.C., to do some sightseeing. The Capitol, the Jefferson and Lincoln Memorials, the White House—it was hard to believe we were actually in America. It would have been even harder to believe the dreams that would come true for us in this land of the free and home of the brave.

"America, the land we love, is still the
land of opportunity and freedom.
We are ever grateful to those who sacrificed
so much so we might have liberty."

ANDY HORNER

"God bless America. Let's not forget
that her greatness is not in her
intellectualism, technology, or natural
resources, but in her people."

ANDY HORNER

CHAPTER FOUR

Deep in the Heart of Texas

I
t was May of 1950 when we crossed into
Texas. It was suddenly very hot, and Joan
loved it. She immediately felt like she
belonged there. Perhaps she had such strong feelings
because God knew this was where we would live and
where Joan would find Him.

NOT JUST A COINCIDENCE

The people in Austin couldn't have been nicer to
three refugees from the far North. Lee Forbes' friends,
the ones Joan knew only by letter writing, gave us a
warm Texas welcome and took us under their wings.
One couple let us live in an apartment on the second
floor of their house, and we set about finding jobs.
Joan found work right away as a bookkeeper at a ladies'
wear store downtown, but I could not find a job anywhere. No one wanted to hire an immigrant. Finally,
after several weeks, I was hired for very low wages to
run a mimeograph machine at the State Highway
Department.

I reported to work the following Monday, and no one was there. I sat on the steps of the government building and tried to figure out why everyone had disappeared. I soon discovered it was a holiday, Memorial Day, and no one had remembered to tell me not to come in to work! Angry and discouraged, I decided that we should drive up to Dallas to go to a baseball game that evening. We found Burnett Field just inside the city limits and got a motel room close by.

A neighbor of ours in Woodstock, Bert Blair, had told us that if we ever got to Dallas, we should call his brother. From the motel Joan started calling all the Blairs in the Dallas phone book, asking them if they had a brother in Canada. An hour later, when she got to the very last Blair—William T.—his wife, Mary, screamed out, "Yes, my husband has a brother in Canada!" We made arrangements to meet them the next morning and then went on to the ball game. (Just for the record, I want it noted that on our first night in Dallas, I took Joan to a baseball game—and I am still doing it sixty years later!)

At 7:30 the next morning, Bill Blair knocked on our door. I told him what had happened in Austin, and he immediately took charge. He took me to get a Social Security card, took me to an employment agency, and got me a job at Gillette Motor Freight. He accomplished all of this before noon! I went back to the motel and asked Joan if she wanted to stay in Dallas, and she immediately said "yes." Bill found us an efficiency apartment to rent, so we were set. We drove down to Austin, packed up our stuff, thanked the friends who had been so generous and kind, and moved to Dallas—just like that.

What a series of coincidences! Joan's strong desire to come to America, the quick stop in Boston, welcomed by strangers in Austin, the futile job search, a trip to Dallas on a whim to see a baseball game, and wham! Suddenly a friend manages to set everything up and gives a young couple that precious gift called opportunity. We never wanted to return to Canada. We never doubted our decision to move to America. And when we landed in Dallas, we knew we were home. Was all this coincidence, or was an unseen hand gently nudging us in His direction?

LEARNING THE BASICS IN THE OFFICE

In Canada I made about eighty dollars a month working three jobs. At Gillette Motor Freight I started at forty dollars a week. Joan and I felt like Texas millionaires. After I'd been working about a month, Bill came by and said that the company where he worked, Allen Engineering, needed an office manager. He thought I should apply for the job. I knew nothing about management. My only experience in an office was at LaFrance Textiles. But Bill said I could do it and he got me hired. This was in July of 1950.

The job at Allen Engineering was the best thing that could have happened to me. It threw me into a crash course in American business, and I was determined to succeed. Like playing athletics as a kid, what I lacked I made up for by plain old hard work. My mother's training paid off. I always did more than I had to, and my bosses noticed. Bill took me under his wing, mentored me, and was proud of everything I accomplished. God partially answered my boyhood prayer for a father in Bill Blair.

I left Allen Engineering after about a year. Mr. Allen was going through a divorce (his third), and the court called me to testify. On the stand I had to say some things that cost my boss more alimony than he wanted to pay. After the trial, I decided it might be best for me to leave. Again it was time to locate another job. The Texas Employment Commission provided a list of possibilities, and I went out on all kinds of interviews. The first one was at a sausage packing factory. What a smell! I learned to thank God for closed doors.

One day at the Employment Commission, I overheard a counselor telling her client about an office manager's job at S. C. Johnson and Son (Johnson Wax) that required a college degree. I had dropped out of high school and had no college credits, but this didn't deter me. I drove to Johnson Wax and interviewed with Mr. Lansford, the regional manager. He told me he was considering a candidate who had a degree from Notre Dame, but he was still making up his mind.

I knew I could handle the job and I wanted it. As I left the building, I introduced myself to all the ladies in the office. Every day I went to check if Mr. Lansford had hired anyone yet, and when I did, I stopped to talk to the women, asking about their families and getting to know them. After about a week of this, Mr. Lansford decided that he would let the women in the office decide who they wanted to be their boss. They unanimously said, "That nice young man from Canada," and I was hired. It pays to pay attention to the working women!

I like to tell this story because I think it demonstrates the power of building relationships. I did not have the experience they wanted or the education they required, but I genuinely liked people and could get along with almost anyone. The ability to relate and to lead was something I worked on even as a boy. I think that this love for people, and my mother's faithful prayers, have been major keys in my success.

Mr. Lansford was demanding, hard to work for, and almost impossible to please. I resented him and decided that he exemplified everything I didn't want to be as a manager. But he taught me many things nobody else had the courage to even mention: "Andy, you stink! Use deodorant!" and "Why don't you wear an undershirt under your dress shirt?" These personal-care issues were things no one told me as a poor kid in Woodstock. Mr. Lansford showed me how to present myself as a businessman, how to run official meetings, and he taught me proper etiquette. He embarrassed me, frustrated me and made me angry, but I discovered that sometimes the people we like the least teach us the most.

DISCOVERING AND RECOVERING SPIRITUAL LIFE

Joan and I began to get established in Dallas. We found a good preschool for Andrea, and Joan got a job with the Reserve Life Insurance Company downtown.

Some of the women she worked with became good friends, especially Marie Hunter. They started talking to their Canadian friend about coming to their church. Still in my backslidden state, church was the last place I wanted to be. Besides, these people were liberal Southern Baptists. I had heard all about their kind in Woodstock—these women wore lipstick and cut their hair. Some of them even smoked! I piously told Joan we shouldn't associate with any of them, but of course the real reason I resisted was that I didn't like the voice that kept speaking to me deep inside. I had been able to stay away from anything having to do with God. The only time I brought Him into the picture was when Joan and I had a fight. I would tell her that I was going to heaven and she was going to hell because she wasn't saved. You can imagine the effect of this kind of witness.

In spite of my objections, Joan liked these ladies and wanted to visit their church. So where do you think we went? I found the biggest Bible I could find and tucked it under my arm. Surely no one would bother me if I carried the family Bible. We found the church and got settled in the pew without incident. But then the pastor got up to welcome the visitors. "We are so honored today to have Brother and Sister Horner here with us from Canada. Brother Horner, would you please come up here and lead us in the invocation?" I couldn't believe it. I gave Joan an elbow and an angry look before I went up front and prayed. I hadn't been in a church for over ten years, but I remembered the art, and the right words came out loud and clear. Andy Horner did his social thing—what a phony.

When we got home, I decided that I would take care of this church thing once and for all. "Joan, no more church! Period! I've had it. I will never darken the door of a church again!" Of course, the women at Joan's work didn't know of my firm words to Joan. They kept right on inviting her to church, and she kept right on accepting their invitations. I lost my temper, but to no avail. When Joan makes a promise, she keeps it. So where do you think I ended up several more times? I made many passionate speeches insisting that our church career was over, but then even the calendar turned against me. It was the Easter season.

Because Joan was a religious person, she was in the habit of going to church on Good Friday and Easter. She knew better than to ask me, so instead she went with her friend Marie to the noon service on Good Friday, led by Dr. W. A. Criswell at the Palace Theater. The service touched Joan deeply, and she cried during most of it. This was the first time she recalls recognizing that something was missing in her life, that something was seriously wrong.

On Easter Sunday, Billy Graham was preaching in Fort Worth. The year before, we had heard him speak in Boston. That time, I went because of mistaken identity. I thought Joan was taking me to see Billy Graham, the prize fighter. In the meantime Billy, the evangelist, had become quite well known, and this was his last weekend in Fort Worth. I could tell that Joan really wanted to go, and since it was Easter, I agreed to take her.

We sat on the top row of the stadium, about as far away as you could get from the speaker, but Billy's message reached us. When he pointed his finger and said, "God is calling you," I felt like he was pointing right at me. Joan was confused. What did Billy mean when he talked about knowing Christ, and why were all these people walking down to the front? I knew what was going on, and all I wanted was to get out of there.

About a month later, in late April, we got a Monday night visit from another of Joan's coworkers, Mrs. Ritchie, a member of First Baptist Church of Dallas. She was an older lady doing church visitation with a gentleman from the church. They came in, sat down and talked with us about their church, their pastor, Dr. Criswell, and how she would love for us to come visit. Just to get her out of my home, I said we might visit sometime. Her response? "Well, how about this Sunday?" I told her that we couldn't make it this Sunday, but maybe some other time. Then Mrs. Ritchie proceeded to explain that this was going to be a very special Sunday. They were having a special convocation and were trying to get as many people to come as possible. Joan thought it was some kind of contest and that our presence could help Mrs. Ritchie win a prize. "We'll be there on Sunday!" she said.

I couldn't believe it. As soon as Mrs. Ritchie left, I told Joan there was no way we were going to that church. I had repeatedly said, "No more church," and that was that. Joan argued back, "But I promised we would be there! We've got to go! It wouldn't be fair to Mrs. Ritchie if we didn't."

The next Sunday morning, April 29, 1951, the telephone woke us up at 7:00 a.m. We had been out late the night before partying, and it was a cool, rainy day—perfect for sleeping in. The call was from Mrs. Ritchie, who was checking to make sure we were coming to church. Joan said, "Yes, of course we are coming." I exploded and gave specific instructions from the other side of the bed. "Joan, make up an excuse, anything, because we are absolutely not going." Mrs. Ritchie, unaware of my frantic objections, offered to come and pick us up. Joan said no, we had a car and would meet her there. We found out later that she had no car. She would have had to borrow one. She was simply determined to eliminate every excuse we made and get us there.

When Joan hung up, the war began. I insisted that we were not going. "I'm the head of the home. No way! We're not going." Joan insisted we were obligated. The battle raged. We climbed out of bed, got dressed and got into the car. Evidently, the Lord had been planning this appointment for quite some time.

We arrived downtown and walked into the First Baptist Church. The place was huge, the largest church I had ever seen. The first thing they did was put Andrea in the nursery. Then they took us into the 2,700-seat sanctuary. Both of us were a little nervous. They whisked Joan away to the women's class on one side of the auditorium, while I went to the men's class on the other. Here we were, separated in this gigantic church, and then Dr. Criswell stood to speak.

He quoted John 3:16 and preached an evangelistic message that morning. He spoke for just ten minutes. It could qualify as his shortest sermon ever. But in those moments he made the Gospel simple and understandable. Clearly and simply, Dr. Criswell revealed God's love and what it meant to simply trust Jesus, what He did on the cross to pay the penalty for our sins, and what it meant that He had risen from the dead. When the invitation started, hundreds began to go down to the front. I was struggling. I knew I had to get right with God, but I kept fighting it. I didn't know where Joan was or what she was thinking about all this, but I started praying, "God, please save Joan. It will be too hard to live for You if she isn't a Christian. If you will just save Joan, then I will submit to You." I stood there praying for Joan, but I knew that I needed to get right with God myself.

Across the auditorium Joan was having her own struggle. She had always been taught that Jesus was the Savior of the whole world, but she didn't understand what His death had to do with her individual life. She was a very religious, moral woman. Why did she need to be forgiven? Why all this talk about sin and separation from God? Why did God's Son have to die?

Dr. Criswell stopped the singing and had everyone get down on their knees and pray. It was then that Joan began to see that her religious performance could never pay the penalty for her sin. She understood that she was separated from God, that Jesus had taken the punishment she deserved, and that now there was something He wanted her to do. She needed to personally respond to Him and accept Him as her Lord and Savior.

Joan told the Lord that she did not want to be apart from Him. She would accept His offer and allow

Him to forgive her and enter her life. Immediately she felt clean. She got up and walked down toward the front, not exactly sure why she was going there.

I had no idea what Joan was doing, but I couldn't hold out any longer. I knew I had to rededicate my life to the Lord, with or without Joan. I moved out into the aisle and began making my way to the front. I came down the right side and the instant I arrived, I saw Joan coming from the left. I walked toward her and we met in the middle. Our lives have been united with Christ since that moment. We were both totally changed.

"If you want favor with both God and man,
and a reputation for good judgment
and common sense, then trust the Lord
completely; don't ever trust yourself."

PROVERBS 3:4-5, TLB

*

"You can be persuaded that whatever we
commit unto the Lord, He is able to keep.
This is a great fact."

ANDY HORNER

CHAPTER FIVE

The Fabulous Fifties

We knew that our lives had definitely changed. Our relationship improved. We still got angry at each other sometimes, but the outbursts of temper with all the yelling, screaming and throwing things at one another ended. Our social calendar definitely changed as our lives became focused on growing in the Lord. Most of our activities began to revolve around First Baptist Church.

SPIRITUAL BABY STEPS AT FIRST BAPTIST

One of the first things Joan wanted to do after she became a Christian was to get baptized. I couldn't understand why she would want to do such a thing or why she thought she needed to. I couldn't talk her out of it and couldn't explain things very well, so I decided that we should meet with Dr. Criswell and talk about it.

We made an appointment and went to his office. He listened to our testimonies and then talked to us about some first steps in our new Christian life. He stressed the importance of obeying Christ, and that the first step of obedience was to be baptized. He told us that Jesus Himself walked miles over rough terrain to the Jordan to set the example. Dr. Criswell said that it must be the Holy Spirit prompting Joan to want to be baptized because she had not been taught about it, had never even seen an adult baptism, and certainly her husband hadn't told her to do this. He told me that I should not hold her back if this is what God was leading her to do.

This meeting with Dr. Criswell was strategic for Joan and me; that was the day he truly became our pastor. His gentle and sweet teaching encouraged us, and we have loved him dearly ever since. He baptized Joan on the following Sunday, May 13, 1951.

We immediately got involved in the programs of First Baptist Church. We joined a Training Union group (that was the Sunday night activity) and got to know a lot of other young couples. We made many lifelong friends and had a great time together. Joan joined a women's Sunday school class that was taught by Mary Crowley. If Dr. Criswell was Joan's spiritual father, Mary Crowley became her spiritual mother. Mary came to our apartment in the afternoons and taught Joan about the Bible. She started at the beginning and took Joan through the Bible chronologically, teaching her the stories and giving her an overview of the Scriptures and of God's plan. Joan had always been an excellent student and she was eager to study. She grew quickly as a Christian.

Mary also taught Joan how to pray. With Andrea down for a nap, Mary and Joan would kneel beside an old chair in our living room. Joan could sense Mary's deep faith, and she learned from Mary that there was nothing too big or too small about which to ask God. One of Joan's first prayer requests was to get pregnant. We had been trying for some time to have a second child but with no success. Then, in May 1952, Sarah was born—proof to us that God does listen and answer our prayers. Once the Lord got started, He just kept pouring on the blessings. Tim was born in December 1953, Mary in April 1956, and Tommy in August 1958. In very short order, we went from one child to five!

On a return trip to Woodstock, Joan learned the source of her spiritual hunger. We were visiting Oxford Street Church, where I had attended for so many years, when a Mrs. Whitehead came up to Joan and asked her if Cecily knew that she had become a Christian. The only Cecily whom Joan knew was Cecily Hardwicke, her nanny from the time she was born until she was six. Mrs. Whitehead said, "Yes, that's the one. You must call her."

Joan went home from church and immediately called Cecily. She identified herself and explained that Mrs. Whitehead told her to call and let her know that she had become a Christian. Sobbing with joy, Cecily said that she had been praying for Joan for thirty years. Joan was amazed as Cecily told her of the choruses she had sung to her, the Bible stories she had told her, and how she had talked about Jesus as she pushed Joan in her stroller. It was clear that God had been at work in

Joan's life since her earliest years through this loving, faithful Christian nanny.

All during this time, our family life and social life revolved around the First Baptist Church. We were active in Sunday school and Training Union, soon taking on teaching and leadership responsibilities. Joan joined a WMU (Women's Missionary Union) circle and attended Bible studies. I was elected to the Junior Board and became a deacon. We went to Sunday morning service, Sunday school, Training Union, Sunday evening service, and Wednesday night prayer meeting. The kids were in Sunday school, Training Union, Sunbeams, GAs (then, Girls' Auxiliary; today, Girls in Action), RAs (Royal Ambassadors), choirs, Vacation Bible School—whatever was going on, we were there, often four and five days a week. At the same time, I was grabbing for the next rungs on the corporate ladder.

A CHANCE FOR THE TOP

These were the 1950s—the days of *Ozzie and Harriet*, *Leave It to Beaver* and *Walt Disney*—and my role as breadwinner was to work hard and keep bringing home a lot more than bacon. I eagerly climbed the corporate ladder at Johnson Wax, honing my skills and making a reputation for myself in the company. My job performance was good, and I was getting very nice raises and bonuses—so much so that in 1952, Joan and I were able to buy a nice three-bedroom home, and in 1956, to build our "dream house" with four bedrooms, two baths, and a family kitchen! Then the big break came.

In early 1959, Mr. Lansford mentioned to me that there was a job opening at company headquarters in Racine, Wisconsin. He thought I was qualified, and he had put my name in for the job. "Andy, you're a talented and motivated young man," he told me. "This is a big opportunity. I think you should pursue it." My head swelled three hat sizes. A job at the Home Office! Here I was, a poor kid from Belfast who started with nothing, living the American dream.

Without much thought and virtually no investigation, I took the promotion and made plans for us to move to Wisconsin. If I had known then what I know now, I would not have been so hasty. I never honestly consulted Joan and certainly didn't seriously consider her or the kids' wishes. To me, and probably to most other men of that era, it was a given that I would grab such an opportunity. This was my goal as a working man. The point was to make it to the top of the company. This proved you were a good provider for your family and a husband any wife would be proud of. And I was on my way!

After getting the promotion, I moved immediately to Racine, leaving Joan in Dallas, pregnant, with five kids, to organize the family move by herself. I threw myself into the important thing—my new job as Assistant to the Marketing Vice President. The headquarters were beautiful and new, designed by Frank Lloyd Wright, and just being there was heady stuff. I was oblivious to any family problems. However, before Joan could move to Racine, she had a miscarriage. In retrospect, I believe that this miscarriage resulted partly from the emotional and physical stress related to having to leave Dallas and organize the move by herself.

Not too many weeks later, I loaded Joan and the kids into the station wagon and moved them to Racine. Joan was still not well. She spent her first few weeks in Wisconsin in the hospital. The kids were crammed into a two-bedroom apartment while our new house was being finished. They were literally living out of boxes and eating on top of them, adjusting to new schools and new friends, all without Joan—and me working my way to the top.

Some wonderful Christian people from the Racine Bible Church saw to it that dinner was provided every night. They helped with the kids, the cleaning and the laundry. Of course, when Joan was home and well enough, the first church we wanted to visit was Racine Bible. We got very involved and had a lot of fun trying to loosen those somber Yankees up, getting them to take some risks as a church, and step out on faith. The pastor, Phil Whisenhunt, had studied at Dallas Theological Seminary and some of Texas had rubbed off on him. We loved him and his family and made many other dear friends. Church and a few friends were the only good things for Joan in the north. She hated the cold, the snow, and the reserve of the people. She was depressed by her surroundings, and she missed Dallas, Dr. Criswell, her friends and the hot weather.

One New Year's, Joan was so homesick that she decided to go to Dallas for Dr. Criswell's New Year's Eve service. We drove to Chicago so she and our three youngest could catch the train, but all the seats were sold. Joan was determined to get there one way or another, so I paid a porter to let her sit in a restroom—and that's where she and the kids rode, all the way to Dallas!

I performed well at Johnson Wax and was promoted again, this time to National Administration Manager. This position gave me more responsibility and placed me on critical management committees. I learned a lot about how corporate managers think and plan, and was exposed to the inner operations of the company. Johnson Wax was a well-organized and well-managed company. It provided a wonderful opportunity to learn valuable management lessons. I learned the importance of company image, and how vital it is to maintain a good company name. They pounded home the message of quality and service, and how hard a company must work to maintain that quality and service.

But there was also a disillusioning side. Some of the luster of corporate headquarters began to fade. I learned how to play corporate games—how to be politic and flatter others. It was my responsibility to write the minutes for the management committee meetings, and I saw how my bosses altered the minutes to say only what they wanted them to say; how they manipulated others to make sure their own positions were secure and to cover up mistakes. I watched—and I learned how to do it, too. I saw myself becoming more like the men I worked for and beginning to violate my own principles. It made me uncomfortable. Working at company headquarters wasn't what I had expected it would be, and it certainly wasn't what I thought it should be. I hardly recognized some of the basic lessons God was teaching me to prepare for what He had planned down the road.

With my growing disillusionment and Joan's persisting unhappiness, I began to think about doing something else. Irishmen can be slow learners, but finally I got the message about how a husband should be more concerned about his wife's needs than his own ego in business. I knew we needed to get out of the cold north and get back home. Joan ran across a newspaper ad for a business for sale in the small east-Texas town of Gladewater and investigated it. I had always dreamed of going into business for myself, and this looked like a good opportunity. It was a little office supply business that was doing well enough to support us. The owner was selling the business and a nice brick house together in one deal. I thought this would be a good place for the kids to grow up. It also got us back to Texas, only two hours from Dallas. I knew Joan would be pleased. I made an offer that the owner, Homer Dennis, accepted. Immediately we made plans to move, while at the same time planning ways to expand the business. I struck a deal with Johnson Wax to carry their complete line of janitorial supplies and in one stroke set up a distribution center for east Texas. "A & J Office and Janitorial Supplies" was born.

A CHANCE FOR OUR OWN BUSINESS

We moved from Racine in the summer of 1962. We

were sad to leave some of the people, but we were also glad to be going home to Texas. We settled into our new home and began establishing roots in the city. We attended the First Baptist Church of Gladewater. Joan was involved in women's clubs and with the kids' schools. I became active in civic clubs and traveled. I spent much of my time on the road drumming up new business for the janitorial supplies, while Joan kept the store going. I was uniquely qualified to be selling janitorial supplies, of course, and did very well at demonstrating how to scrub and wax floors. I'd had years of practice at my mother's knee—literally!

The business slowly grew, and our selling radius expanded. But I had never worked so hard for so little in my life. Joan and I were both putting in sixty-plus-hour weeks and we were getting tired. We also didn't have much time for a decent family life, and we missed that. The only way we could get any time off was to hang a sign on the door saying we were at a funeral. Members of our families died in droves during those two years—some even died twice!

A CHANCE TO RETURN TO BIG D

Although we were back in Texas, a huge improvement, Joan still longed to live in Dallas and return to the First Baptist Church and her pastor. She missed Dr. Criswell's preaching and wanted the kids involved in the programs at First Baptist. We occasionally drove the eighty miles to Dallas on Sundays to go to church and see friends. This only made her miss it more.

In early 1963, Joan was again up to her practice of

placing newspaper ads on my dresser. This time the ad was for a job with the Xerox Corporation. They were building a new regional distribution center and were looking for a manager. Guess where they wanted to place this center? Now I knew nothing about Xerox. In fact, I thought it was the antifreeze company. But I sent in my resume anyway, just for the fun of it, and then forgot about it.

Months later, I was surprised when I received a call from Andy Price of Xerox. It took me a few seconds to realize what he was calling about. He asked me to drive to Dallas and interview for the position I had applied for months earlier. I figured I had nothing to lose, so I did the interview. I was called back for two more interviews over the next three months. I was tested and evaluated by the company psychologist, Dr. Smith. He and I developed a wonderful relationship, and he was very helpful in many ways. He helped me to understand myself better and to see why I did the things I did. He helped me see that I needed to relax and accept the fact that everyone has weaknesses, including me, and there was no need to try to hide them. He also counseled that probably I would be happier as a big fish in a little pond, than as a little fish in a big pond. Despite getting to know me so well, he must have decided I wasn't too crazy because I was offered the job in the fall of 1963.

Joan and I decided that I should take the position. She remained in Gladewater running the business until it sold. I moved up to Irving and lived in a rented house until the family joined me in January of 1964.

Xerox was a good company and the job was an excellent opportunity. I oversaw the completion of the new Dallas distribution center and organized the warehousing and distribution of parts and equipment for the entire Southwest. This kind of task was right up my alley, and I liked the challenge of it. During these years, Xerox was growing and expanding rapidly. My region kept up so well with the growth that I was sent to other distribution centers in the United States and in Canada to analyze the organization and come up with recommendations to improve operations. It was exciting.

Of course, not everything about any job is all good. One of the drawbacks to working at Xerox at this time was that such rapid growth brought frequent changes in policy. Every time a new person became president or vice president of some division, things changed. Sometimes the changes came down so fast that it was hard to keep up. We would be in the process of implementing one set of changes as another new set was handed down. Projects would be canceled with no warning and no explanation. Once, we were in the process of opening a machine replacement center in Dallas. We had leased the building and hired the staff, only to be told that the center was being shut down. We were closed down before we even opened up! I have to admit that this Irishman got frustrated more than once.

In general, though, I was happy. My job was good and taught me one very important lesson: It is vital to support your product and serve your customers if you want to sustain growth. I saw time and time again how Xerox beat the competition because we could service the customer better, quicker and more efficiently. My experience convinced me that serving and supporting were the keys, a principle that I have never forgotten. Was it just by chance that I found myself working for a company that skillfully drove this lesson deep into my heart?

After a few years, I had the distribution center running so efficiently that I ended up with a lot of time to play golf and get bored. Now I hate doing nothing, because you never know when you're done. I looked to other challenges instead and got involved in various civic organizations. I was elected president of the Rotary Club and chaired the Community Chest drive. Xerox encouraged their managers to do these kinds of things, so they were pleased and I enjoyed it.

Years earlier, Johnson Wax had encouraged me to continue my education, and had paid for me to attend classes two or three nights a week at Southern Methodist University in Dallas. My college degree was on hold when we moved to Racine, but now back in Dallas, I pursued my education again. I had never thought of myself as college material, and I am sure that my teachers and principals in Canada never did either. This was one time my "hyperactivity" was a positive thing. It gave me energy to burn and an ability to do several things all at once. Because of my hectic schedule, I needed help. My college degree was a family affair. Without Joan's support and my daughter Andrea's tutoring, I would not have made it. I graduated from college the same day Andrea graduated from high school.

Joan and I again immersed ourselves at First Baptist and maintained a breakneck pace of activities and raising our five kids. The kids were into everything—church, school and especially sports. We enjoyed getting to be a part of it all. We tried our best never to miss a performance or a game. We also were back to teaching Sunday school and leading a Training Union department. We developed outreach ministries in our neighborhood. Joan taught two Bible study classes a week—one for young married women and one for more mature women—and we had a couples' Bible class in our home once a week for our neighbors, nicknamed the "Humble-ites." Combine all this with a monthly dinner club with church friends, along with extensive camping and boating, and you've got a very active social and family calendar.

These were great years, but they were also too busy. Often I felt tired and weary. At times I felt like quitting everything. The Horners are a wandering, rootless group by nature, and the temptation was there. If it were not for Joan and the five kids, I think I might have drifted away. But the responsibility of a wife, five children and a home kept me disciplined at my work. I certainly didn't have much internal peace or joy, but I stayed with it regardless of how I felt. Dads and husbands weren't supposed to quit in the 1950s and 1960s. Feeling fulfilled and discerning my life purpose, however, would have to wait for more maturing.

"Although your road may bend and curve,
And winds blow hard that can disturb,
Keep moving on and you will find
More opportunities and much sunshine."

ANDY HORNER

✻

"Difficulties and problems in life can either
be stumbling blocks or stepping stones, but
are always opportunities for growth."

ANDY HORNER

CHAPTER SIX

The Direct Sales Connection

f the Horner tribe possessed some wanderlust genes, the mid-1960s gave me a lot of temptation to activate them. I did, in fact, make an important journey from *wax* to *copiers* to *home decorating*, but it all happened right in Dallas.

FROM COPIERS TO HOME DECORATING

Because of my success in organizing the Dallas distribution center, Xerox began offering me other positions and promotions outside of Dallas. But I had learned a lesson—not all that glitters on the corporate staircase to success is gold. I decided I would not move my family again unless all of us agreed.

In 1966, Xerox offered me a job at their corporate headquarters in Rochester, New York. Frigid winds off Lake Erie, piles of snow and the necessity of moving across the Mason-Dixon Line—Joan wanted nothing to do with it, and the kids agreed. The Johnson Wax headquarters experience had taught me that a relocation was not necessarily a trip to heaven. But I also knew that if I kept turning down this kind of promotion, my career at Xerox would be placed on hold. Rejecting promotions just wasn't done. It put lack of loyalty, no ambition, and questionable commitment on your resume. I knew that I would no longer be considered a "company man," and the offers would soon stop. I also worried that my job in Dallas might be in jeopardy. I went ahead and turned it down and wondered what the future would hold. At least I had finally learned to put my family ahead of my career. It was about time.

I was surprised when, only a few months later, the company offered me another promotion. Xerox was diversifying into other businesses and had recently acquired a book distribution operation on the West Coast. They asked me to move to California and head up this new division. Ocean and beaches, skiing and surfing, Disneyland and plenty of sunshine—this time Joan and the kids were interested! Joan and I took a couple of trips to California and hunted for houses. We discovered one with a beautiful pool and checked out the nearby churches. We all felt we could be happy there, and everyone was in agreement that this was a good move, so I accepted the position. My replacement was hired and moved to Dallas with his family. I trained him, and we prepared to move to the land of the fruits and the nuts.

I can't believe what happened next. I had accepted the new position, we were packing our things to move, and I was training my replacement; but I had no excitement about the new position. My enthusiasm was zero, and I couldn't sleep at night. I just had no peace about the whole thing. Joan and I did a lot of late-night talking and praying. What in the world was going on with me? Everything was in place for us to go, but I just didn't feel like going. Joan and I decided that if I felt this way, we shouldn't move.

I called company headquarters and told them I had changed my mind. I told them that I had decided to stay in Dallas and not take the California job after all. I didn't know how they would react, but they generously offered me my old job back. I stayed on, but decided that it would be wise to start looking for a job with a Dallas-based company. I didn't ever want to face the prospect of moving again!

THE HOME INTERIORS EXPERIENCE

One of my friends suggested that I talk to Mary Crowley, who knew many business people and might know of some openings in Dallas. Joan and I remembered Mary, of course. In our early years in Dallas, she had been Joan's Sunday school teacher and had helped Joan take her first steps of growth in the Lord. We loved and respected her deeply, but we had lost touch with her. I didn't even know she had her own company, Home Interiors and Gifts. I thought that it wouldn't hurt to get back in contact with her and see if she might know of some open doors.

I made an appointment and went to Mary's office. It was good to see her again and we had a pleasant, relaxed conversation. "Andy, give me some of your background and tell me what you would like to do now." I ran through my job history and told her that I was hoping she might be able to give me some referrals. Her next words stunned me. Out of the blue she said, "Andy, I believe you are God's man for Home Interiors. You need to be right here with us."

Mary's words caught me totally off guard. I didn't know what to say. I hadn't even considered this possibility. Besides, I wasn't sure at all that I was the man for her job. This was a direct sales company with about ten thousand women Displayers (independent contractors) selling home-decorating accessories. I knew nothing about direct sales or home accessorizing, and I wasn't sure I wanted to get involved in a business with ten thousand women! But Mary insisted that I at least talk to her son, Don Carter, about the possibility of coming to work with them. I agreed to do that much.

Mary set up the appointment, and I arrived right on time. I sat there—waiting and waiting and waiting. After over an hour, I was impatient and frustrated. I believed I knew the scenario: Don's mother was probably making him talk to me, and he did not share her belief that I was needed at Home Interiors. When we finally spoke, I got the distinct feeling that he wasn't interested in talking with me about anything. We had a very short visit, and I got up and left. The Horner pride still needed some downsizing.

Mary was in Europe during this botched appointment episode. When she heard what had happened, she sent me an airgram asking me not to make any decision until she got back. She reconfirmed that she was sure that I was God's man for Home Interiors. By the time she returned I had begun applying for other jobs, but Mary would not let it go. She was the most persistent and determined lady I have ever known. She stayed on me, even visiting our home to try and convince me. When she got to our place, she looked around and said, "Why all these blank walls? A home just should not be this empty! Your walls need some loving." The next thing I knew, she was back with boxes full of decorating items. She completely accessorized our house! And it was awesome. I saw firsthand what a difference accessories could make in a home. She had convinced me about her product and the service she offered. As she continued to talk with me, I was also intrigued by the direct sales angle and Mary's philosophy of business.

Still, a major doubt lingered. How would I fit in with a mother-son leadership team? I just didn't see Home Interiors in my future. However, Mary wouldn't take no for an answer. She asked me in July of 1967 if I would come in the evenings after my workday at Xerox to do what I could to help out.

Just as Mary had thought, there was some room for improvement. The sales organization was doing fine and was growing rapidly. But because of the rapid growth in the field, the warehouse and home office systems were lagging behind, unable to service and support the field the way it deserved. It was apparent that if they didn't get those elements in line, the continued growth of the company was in jeopardy.

After about six months, I received a call from Don asking if he could meet with me. I agreed, but this time I had him come to my Xerox office. I certainly wasn't going to sit again for an hour in his waiting room! Our visit went well. We talked about the growth and expansion of Home Interiors and what kind of things needed to be done to ensure the future. He told me about the family atmosphere of their company and how it differed from Xerox or other corporations. I didn't know where he was coming from that day, but many years later he told me that his mom was so excited about the possibility of getting me that she just didn't let up on him. She told him to go out to Xerox to hire me before someone else snatched me, and even to buy some copier machines in order to get me to come on board! It was his mother's confidence and "feeling of joy about it" that convinced him, he said. He and Mary made me an offer, and I began full-time with Home Interiors in early 1968. Don told me at the time that this would be the best decision I ever made in my life. He was right.

And what about that job in California? The new division that I was to have managed for Xerox was consolidated with a company based in Detroit, Michigan! I believe that there was Someone who loved us very much who gave me those sleepless nights and uneasy feelings. He protected us from a potentially disastrous, short-lived move to the West Coast because He had some very special things in store for us at Home Interiors.

I started at Home Interiors as Don Carter's assistant, overseeing the warehouse and taking over various administrative and organizational duties for Don.

I never worked so hard in my life—and I have done a lot of hard work. There was a lot of pressure keeping up with the growing sales force. To add to the stress, I was working for a mother and her son. I tried to please them both, but it was sometimes difficult. I was middle management all right—right in the middle between Mary and her son. At times it was a difficult situation for me, and after only a few months, I thought I had made a big mistake.

I considered quitting many times, but I have never felt right about running away from something difficult. Plus, the money was good. We had one child in college by then and four close behind her. Like most men in midlife, my family responsibilities made me stay, although it was an emotional roller coaster ride the entire seventeen years I was there. God doesn't promise us a relaxing vacation on Waikiki Beach. He had some important lessons for me to learn in the midst of this struggle.

The Mary Crowley School of Wisdom

Mary Crowley worked hard and demanded the same of others, but she was also extremely generous. She always had a moment to look you in the eye, take you by the hand, and ask how you were. She was thoughtful and loving, strong and straightforward, with an unwavering faith in God. Mary firmly believed that everybody is a somebody. I can still hear her say, "Andy, you be sure to spread this truth. Tell everybody that they are a somebody; that they can do whatever they set their mind to do. God did not take time to make a nobody." Mary insisted that we see others with eyes of love no matter how difficult and negative they were. "We should always see the person as God sees them, a valued child of God, the person they might be able to become, not necessarily the way they are at this moment."

Mary practiced what she preached. She had a way of looking at you and immediately seeing all that you could do and become. Then she challenged you to do and to become just that. "Think mink," she said, "not rabbit or fox or squirrel. Aim for the best. Attempt great things. Believe big and you'll get big results."

Mary taught me to constantly focus on the people. She told me many times, "Andy, if you build the people, they will build the business. Expect the best from them and they will respond. Meet their needs and they will support you and meet every need in your life." She believed that if you helped other people get what they wanted out of life, then you would get what you wanted out of life. She persistently built this sense of "otherness" into the sales force and all the employees. She taught us how to be alert to the needs of others and how serving others meant more than teaching them about home-decorating accessories. "Service is our survival kit. We need to give service in home decorating, but we also need to allow women to air their problems, express their hopes and fears, and help them in whatever ways we can. We will find our highest fulfillment not in beautifying homes but in beautifying lives."

Mary's belief in serving went beyond the customers and the people who did the work. She applied this service to the home office management team. As I worked with her over the years, she transformed my thinking from a *managing others* point of view to a *serving others* point of view. She demonstrated this attitude wherever she went, and I could see the power of it. The more I relaxed and concentrated on ways to serve others and help others, rather than trying to get them to do what I wanted, the better things went for me with people in the field and around the home office. This change in my attitude was needed the most in my relationship with Don and Mary, and I discovered that a spirit of genuine humble service was the key.

Before I met Mary, I had always been a people person. But I learned even more about the way people really are from Mary Crowley. She taught me to genuinely appreciate others and to understand that they are the key to success. "People are our most important asset!" she repeated over and over until this hardheaded Irishman got the message into his life.

There's a story about Mary that demonstrates the priority of people over profits. At the end of her first year of business the company was not going to make a huge profit, but it was not in the red either. She decided that she would pay a small dividend on the stock and give bonuses to the home office staff and managers. She called her accountant and told him to draw up the checks. He was appalled and told her that she could not do this, that if she did, she would have no reserve whatsoever. He said that no one expects a dividend or a bonus the first year of a business. Mary replied, "What do you mean we'd have no reserve? It all depends on what you call reserve. *You* say it's money. *I* say it's people." She paid the dividend and the bonuses, and the company went on to increased profits every year after that. Mary understood that people were the key. Investments in people always pay off. In fact, I developed a little motto for Home Interiors: "To most companies, P & L means Profit and Loss. At Home Interiors, it means People and Love."

Partners on the Road

After a short while, I was promoted to Vice President of Administration and was given some very nice bonuses for the work I was doing. Things were running smoothly. We had the systems in place to serve and support the field the way we wanted to, which in turn led to increases in sales, recruiting and company profits.

In the early 1970s, Mary and Don noticed that there were some areas of the country that were having special problems and needed extra help. They asked me to travel to these areas and do training, leadership development, and rebuilding. Soon I was doing that kind of work exclusively and was given the title to match: Vice President of People and Area Development.

Joan traveled with me whenever she could. Our kids were grown and out on their own, so she was free to leave home. She was an incredible asset to me personally, as well as to the company. The people loved her, and she developed close, supportive relationships with many of our Displayers and managers in the field. She also began assisting Mary in ways that only a good friend could, to the point of accompanying her on many trips both here and abroad.

By 1976, Joan's role had become so vital that Mary and Don asked her to join Home Interiors on a full-time basis. I was pleased, of course, because I had gotten to the place where I refused to travel without her. We made a good team as we worked with the women in the field. Of all the jobs that I had had up to this point, this was the best fit. Both Joan and I loved developing people and building these new sales areas. We were using all our people skills and saw immediate results where they counted—in the lives of women. I watched their confidence and self-esteem grow as they built their businesses. I saw them develop as leaders and as women. This was gratifying work, but it was not easy. It was demanding and exhausting. We worked long hours and traveled almost weekly across the country. Some days I felt absolutely drained, not wanting to take another phone call or get on another plane. But, then, nothing worthwhile is easy.

A BLOWOUT ON THE ROAD

Looking back on those years now, I can hardly believe all that we were doing in addition to our Home Interiors work. We continued to be involved in many ministries at First Baptist Church. We taught Sunday school and led Training Union. I was a deacon and board member. I ushered at many services and often gave the invocation. In the mid-1960s I served on the committee that set up the Criswell Bible Institute, and over the next two decades, I lent whatever leadership and assistance I could. Criswell Bible Institute evolved into the Criswell Center for Biblical Studies and then, ultimately, to its present status of the Criswell College. I served on its Board of Trustees for numerous terms and as Board Chairman twice. I was on the original committee that set up KCBI, the college's Christian radio station, and stayed involved until that ministry was firmly on its feet.

All of these activities were good and worthwhile in themselves, but I was doing them for the wrong reasons and I was wearing myself out "working for Jesus." I equated spirituality with activity. I thought that being a good Christian meant I should be at church every time the doors opened and should serve in whatever capacity I was asked. I didn't comprehend that being a Christian was about a relationship with God, not about a life overly full of Christian activities. I had spent my entire adult life performing for God, and I was getting worn out. I could have received an Academy Award for my role as outstanding, devoted, hard-working Christian and church member, but inside I was hurting and searching for an answer. There was no joy in any of it for me, and the God that created the world in six days was not that impressed.

I was empty, frustrated and burning out as a Christian, and I didn't know what to do about it. I thought about standing in front of our church and yelling out, "Hey, folks, I'm tired. I'm weary. I've lost my joy and my peace. I'm not what you think, and I'm so tired of performing as a Christian. I can't do this anymore. I thought Jesus said His yoke was easy. Pulling this load is killing me!"

To increase the burden, the pressures at Home Interiors were building. Delicate interpersonal and legal problems had to be handled, and the situation was stressful. Many days I whispered to myself, *I've got to resign.* But how could I walk away from the big money and the freedom and security I believed it brought? How could Joan and I stop giving so much support to the various missions and ministries that we loved? There were still the children's college bills to pay. Plus, Joan and I enjoyed working together. She was as involved and attached to the people as I was, and she didn't want to leave them or Mary Crowley. I went to Mary on a number of occasions and tried to resign, explaining that I thought maybe I wanted to pursue full-time Christian work. Each time she told me that I could help others ten times more by giving money to support a number of ministries than I could by going into one ministry myself. Every time I brought up quitting, she talked me out of it. So I stayed and the strain continued to mount.

Our company had experienced world-class growth. Its field leadership was the best in direct sales, from my perspective. They were dedicated and loyal, hard workers. Everyone in business knows that growth brings changes. It demands more structure and administration. It demands a lot more time just to keep pace with the growth and the avalanche of training, motivating and keeping sales and deliveries together. But these structural changes were not what made me want to leave.

From my perspective, our company was losing sight of its original founding principles. I saw us gradually moving away from being a people-oriented business to a profit-oriented business. Our bottom line began to move from the value of people to the value of dollars. Most of our leaders would have denied it, but I sensed the beginning of a slow leak that would, in the end, deplete our core values.

No one had the unique abilities that our founder, Mary Crowley, possessed. She was a dynamic Christian, and she lived and breathed her belief in people—their worth and gifts. When she looked at an individual, she didn't see what they were, but what they could become. I can still hear her say, "Yes, you can and will do great things." And most of the time, they did. Mary focused on the eternal value of an individual. She built her company on the belief that people are our greatest asset, but as we grew, things started to drift. Some of our leaders did not internalize our founder's commitment to people as our greatest strength, and this started to generate a consistency problem.

INCONSISTENCY BETWEEN WORDS AND ACTIONS

When you are faced with a choice between what you know to be right and what is clearly wrong, you must choose the right no matter what the cost. As my responsibilities increased at Home Interiors, I faced a conflict between what was being said in public and what was actually happening in private. The practice did not match the preaching. This is the tough part for all of us Christians in business. We can talk a good game, but it is much harder to live it in the marketplace. So, what do you do when you feel there are inconsistencies in the company where you work?

I did talk to my leaders about the problems, but

when I didn't get much response, I did not act decisively against what I felt to be wrong. My failure to act left me angry, weary and depressed. Because of the stress—much of it self-imposed—I stopped enjoying going to work. Things that had never bothered me before started to bother me. I'm sure that those who worked with me at the time noticed my change in attitude—our associates always do—but I continued the charade.

I was weary, depressed and confused. We should expect our jobs to cause some stress, and sometimes this can be an asset. It keeps the adrenaline high and helps us maintain a healthy competitive edge, like in sports. But when the pressure of the job becomes "distress," it feels like we are drowning with heavy weights attached to our bodies, dragging us down into the depths.

Never have I revealed the specific acts that caused the conflict in Home Interiors while I worked there, and that is not my purpose here. I want to focus, instead, on the importance of integrity—making sure that our walk matches our talk—and the need to act when you believe integrity has been compromised. I felt there were problems in this area, but instead of acting to do something about it or making the decision to leave, I got caught in a vise of indecision. I loved my job and the people I had worked with for years. Many had become special friends.

THE DECISION TO LEAVE

I remember that it had been a long day at work. I was driving home alone. It was dark. The thoughts kept running through my head: "Enough is enough! I can't keep doing this! There are serious issues in our company that I have talked to my leaders about, but it goes nowhere. They don't get it. Nothing changes to fix the problem. A lot of people could get hurt if things don't change!" Then my mind would counter: "But there are so many good things about the job. Our company was founded on Christian principles. I have had incredible opportunities in this company. I love so many of the associates I work with, and many of them are friends. Joan and I have had incredible times traveling around the country training our field team! I have an important title and a good income!" As it had many times before, the debate raged in my head: *Should I stay or should I go?*

That night I was home alone. Joan had gone away for a couple of days, and the rest of my family was out of pocket. In despair and depression, I was looking for relief. For two years, I had wrestled with the same problem. And during the last few months, I had started to blame the Lord for the mess. He knew what was going on. Why didn't He do something about it? I started to doubt that He would, or even could, do anything. I was fifty-eight years old with financial security, a wonderful wife and family. I should have been on top of the mountain, but instead I was in a valley—a valley so deep, the darkness separated me from God. I was one miserable person.

My struggle with God and my struggle with integrity and truth at my job had gotten me totally out of sync. My life was out of balance. It was a turning point. I could allow the war to continue and self-destruct, or

I could humbly admit to God what was going on and start to move under His guidance, like a child, toward a solution.

Oh, how I wish I had talked everything over with the Lord sooner, listened to what He had to say, and had the courage to act on His instruction. Finally—that night as I hit bottom—He did step in, and I listened and decided to resign. In 1982, I went to Mary and resigned, telling her that I was emotionally depressed and physically exhausted. For the next year, Joan and I continued to work with a few areas of the country, but as independent consultants to Home Interiors, not employees. In 1984, we made the final break. I was totally burned out and simply couldn't find the energy to continue in any capacity.

I started my own consulting company, Management and People Services, and developed a few clients, providing organizational, training and motivational services to direct sales companies. I felt relieved to be away from the pressure, but the last few years had taken their toll. Desperate and adrift, I struggled with myself and wrestled with God. Now what? Where do I go from here? I was losing hope and started seeking answers in every way I knew how.

*"Don't let feelings determine your destiny.
Most of the work in the world is done
by people who don't feel like it."*

ANDY HORNER

*"Luck in business is equal to preparation
plus hard work plus opportunity."*

ANDY HORNER

CHAPTER SEVEN

The Birth of Premier Designs

As Joan and I were breaking away from Home Interiors, I began pulling away from the church. For a couple of years I just didn't go. I was totally burned out and simply didn't have the fuel to continue. I resigned my positions and withdrew from my teaching responsibilities. I was miserable, discouraged and adrift. Lost in a deep emotional bog, I questioned my faith. I questioned God. Where was He? What was faith? What did I believe?

I cringed at the thought that someone might find out that I was actually asking these kinds of questions. People respected me as a fine Christian and church leader. I couldn't let them know I was actually doubting the truth of the whole thing. I couldn't admit to anyone what was really going on inside. No one knew how bad it was or how low I went. Some days I felt so hopeless and weary I just didn't want to go on.

Then gradually, as I cried out to God for answers, the light began to dawn. I began to realize the truth. I had been sweating it out for Jesus all those years, doing everything I could in my own strength to earn His pat on my head and to hear Him say, "Well done!" In fact, it became clear to me that my major concern had been what people thought of me and whether or not they considered me a good Christian. My focus had been horizontal instead of vertical, and there is nothing more futile than trying to do a supernatural task in plain old natural strength. The phoniness destroyed my inner joy. For many years, I didn't realize this and wondered why my Christian life lacked authenticity. I had worked so hard to please God that I had forgotten to love Him and to let Him love me! Finally, He decided it was time to enroll me in His course on *Son Dependence,* instead of *Andy Dependence.*

Amazing things began to happen over the next year as I spent time studying the Bible and concentrating on my relationship with God. I began opening up with friends, and God provided help and encouragement through them. For example, Bob and Amy George, dear friends and founders of Dallas-based People to People Ministries, reminded me over and over again that God is not interested in our performance, but loves us as we are. I began to rest and relax as I allowed Jesus to work through me, instead of me working for Him.

I stopped asking internal questions like, "What will the church leaders think of me if I do this?" and started asking, "What does my heavenly Father really want?" Step by step, I started seeing small evidences of His Spirit's fruit in my life. Gradually, peace and joy began to reappear in my heart. It was wonderful—revolutionary! I realized that for sixty years God had tried to get me to relax and let Him sculpt me into what He wanted. But my pride made me resistant clay. I was so busy impressing others with my "spirituality" that I lost sensitivity to the Spirit. It took sixty years for God to really get my full attention. I regret that it took so long, but I am grateful that He never gave up on me. Isn't it wonderful to know that God never quits on one of His kids?

During this time of growing close to the Lord, I started asking God to reveal what He wanted me to do with the rest of my life. I didn't need to work for money, but I did need to work for Him. Besides, I don't believe in retirement. The word should be removed from the dictionary. Heaven is God's retirement center, and it is a lot more plush than Palm Springs or Sarasota. I wasn't about to look for shells in the morning on the beach and then play golf all day until a favorite TV sitcom came on that night. I knew God wanted me to change direction, not retire, and to accomplish a whole new mission. But what direction should I take? This time I wanted Him to take the lead.

THE DOOR BEGINS TO OPEN

During this period of searching, I was trying to decide if Joan and I should go into full-time ministry. My brother Hugh was a preacher, and I hoped that God would give me that "special call" to be a preacher, too; but it never came. Joan and I thought about going to the mission field or working with a mission organization in some capacity, but no opportunity opened up.

About this same time, two significant things happened. First, in August 1984, I went on a mission trip to Poland with my friend Dave Wyrtzen, founder of Truth Encounter and pastor of Midlothian Bible Church. We met Dave and his wife, Mary, in 1971, when he was a student at Dallas Theological Seminary. On our flight across the Atlantic from New York to Poland, I had twenty-four hours to finally open up and share with a close friend—someone not connected with my job—about my situation. I shared that I was seeking God's leading and was thinking about becoming a preacher or going to the mission field. But as Dave heard my life experience, he challenged me to take a hard look at my unique personal gifts. "Andy, it's obvious. You're an entrepreneur. In both the corporate world and the world of direct sales, you have received specialized training in how to build a company and how to effectively manage it. Do you think the Lord wants to trash all these skills He has carefully matured in you? Why don't you consider being an entrepreneur for the Lord, a businessman who lives in the marketplace totally at the beck and call of His Master?" *An entrepreneur for Jesus*—the idea intrigued me. This conversation with Dave turned out to be pivotal.

The second major influence came when my daughter Sarah and her family moved to Bolivia, South America, as missionaries. Joan and I went to visit them for Christmas in 1984. While we were there, Bob and Ann Moore invited us to come farther south with them to visit Word of Life Ministries in Argentina.

Joan and I had met Bob and Ann several years earlier through our good friends Bruce and Maggie Peterson—and we had met Bruce and Maggie through our dear friends and neighbors from Racine, Don and Marion Placko. Each summer the Plackos attended a Bible conference at Word of Life headquarters in Schroon Lake, New York. For years, they tried to get us to go with them. Finally, in 1974, we were able to go and we loved it. It was there that we became close friends with Bruce and Maggie, and then Bob and Ann. (Though she hates to admit it, Joan says that the Lord was at work even in our move to Racine— where we met the Plackos, who introduced us to Word of Life! This, as you will see, set off a chain of events that changed our course.)

At that particular time, the last thing we wanted to do was to go to Argentina. Joan was ill, and we were planning to cut the Bolivia visit short and go home early. But Bob kept calling and asking us to come. They said that we just had to come down to see Word of Life work among young people in Argentina. Finally, we gave in and went to a small village outside Buenos Aires. What we saw there radically changed our view of missions. We fell in love with Argentina and felt an immediate affinity for the people. We were impressed by the effectiveness of the national Christians and what they were trying to accomplish. As we saw their needs, we felt an urgent, intense burden to help them. By the time we left, we had committed to building two housing complexes for married couples who wanted to come to the Bible Institute to study. The buildings were named *Doña Juana* and *Doña Sarah* (after Joan and my mother.)

From that time on, Joan and I knew what our role was to be: We were to use our entrepreneurial, managerial and administrative abilities to generate funds— money that could be used to help others. We saw clearly that we could do more for the cause of missions by helping these nationals than by going ourselves. Our full-time ministry was to generate the funds needed to carry out the task of proclaiming the Good News about Christ. But where could we find a business that we could buy and build with the purpose of supporting missions?

When I returned from Argentina, I got a call from my accountant, Wendell Judd, asking me to take a consulting job with a direct selling jewelry company. I knew nothing about jewelry, but I did know a lot about the inner workings of a direct sales company, and Wendell knew from their books that they needed help. They were in serious trouble.

Joan and I went over to their offices and met with them. They had beautiful offices and surroundings, and forty thousand distributors on their rolls. I worked with them for several weeks, trying to help find a way to salvage their company. At one time they had done very well and professed to be a Christian company. I hated to see the company fold. As I looked at their operations, I began thinking, maybe this was a company we could buy and build. I knew direct sales and thought that jewelry would be a harmless enough product to sell.

I sent my attorney to investigate the company with an eye to purchasing it. Every place he looked, he found more dishonesty and trouble. They did not practice what they preached. There were unpaid sales taxes, unpaid commissions, and only one-tenth of their sales force was actually working. They were forty thousand strong on paper, but only four thousand strong in the field. The company was a total disaster, and our attorney counseled that under no circumstances should we purchase this company. They even offered to give it to us if we assumed their debt, but our lawyer said no.

I was furious with him. My heart was set on acquiring this company. Why was he trying to block this perfect means of fulfilling the dream the Lord had given me? I knew that God wanted us involved. But the Bible says that "in [a] multitude of counselors there is safety" (Proverbs 24:6, KJV), so I listened. The Lord was working in my life, because for once I didn't just bull my way forward. I followed our lawyer's truthful, wise counsel and reluctantly broke off all association with the company. It's a good thing I did. If I had not, there would be no Premier Designs, because I would still be trying to untangle that company's royal mess! On the other hand, if I had not consulted with that company to begin with, there would be no Premier Designs, because it was through this contact that the Lord opened the door into the direct selling jewelry industry.

Now, I don't want to give you the impression that I see visions and hear supernatural voices in the night.

Actually, I'm quite normal and don't rely a lot on feelings in my spiritual life. Certainly I have feelings, but faith is much more important to me. No, I have never had an angel appear or had a room light up with bright lights. But a few times—maybe four in all—since I came out of my valley of despair, God has spoken quietly to my heart.

One night I woke up in the middle of the night. For some reason I couldn't get back to sleep. When this happens, I generally talk to God, praying and thanking Him for all His love and blessings. But this night was different. I got into a discussion with God. In the quiet stillness I sensed an unusual closeness and said to God, "I do want to serve You and support Your work, but I *don't* want to go back into direct sales. I just can't do it."

"Andrew" (God does know us by name), "I have been waiting forty years for you to tell me you can't do it. Now let *me* do it." This may sound strange to you, but I must tell you that it was real, and that night I said, "Lord, okay, I'll let you do it!"

THE PREMIER IDEA

Three or four months later two former executives of that now bankrupt jewelry company called and asked if we had found a company yet. Obviously, they were out of work and were fishing in some new waters. Joan and I met with them, and this meeting triggered the idea of starting our own direct selling jewelry company.

I was not too excited about this possibility. When

I left Home Interiors, I vowed never to be involved in a direct sales company again. I was burned out on it. Direct sales was at the bottom of my list of things God might lead us to do. (Being beach missionaries in Hawaii was at the top.) The reputation of many direct sales companies could compete with that of a crooked politician or a TV evangelist. Too many had not kept their promises, and many good people had been hurt. I did not want to be associated with this industry any more.

Then I remembered my middle-of-the-night conversation with the Lord. As I made intimacy with Him my top priority, as I daily allowed Him to talk to me through His Word, and as I talked to Him frequently in prayer, He gave me this solid feeling inside that He wanted me to start this company for Him. For two years, He had sent me on a reconnaissance tour of the needs in the mission field, and now He wanted me to do something about it. We were to start a company and make money to meet those needs.

Joan and I spent several weeks in prayer and discussions with our most trusted advisors. I met with some who questioned my desire and who told me that 1985 was not a good time to start a company, that direct sales were on the decline and there was too much uncertainty ahead. But we met with others who encouraged us. One particular incident stands out in my mind. Drs. Hazel and Howard Goddard, mature Christians and longtime friends and counselors, dropped by our house unexpectedly one evening. We spent the entire time talking about what Joan and I were considering—starting a company at age sixty!

They listened carefully, asked wise questions, and then enthusiastically said, "Go for it!" (Ever since, Hazel, founder of Christian Counseling Ministries, has been one of our most trusted advisors, and Howard was a faithful Prayer Partner and our first Premier Designs chaplain.)

After much thought and prayer, we did decide to "go for it!" We were excited! We could see that God was weaving forty years of business and personal experience into a beautiful whole, offering us an opportunity to put our beliefs, our principles and all of our skills into practice. We would start a direct selling jewelry company built on a foundation of integrity and honesty; one whose most important asset would always be people. Joan and I would fund the company and establish our God-inspired Philosophy, Purpose and way of doing business. The profits would be shared with our employees, Independent Distributors (Jewelers) and ministries in the United States and around the world. Our new executives would provide their experience in jewelry direct sales and run the company with us.

THE BEGINNING

Premier was incorporated on November 5, 1985, in the upstairs office of our home on Red Cedar Trail in Dallas. We began operations on January 20, 1986, with a staff of six people, including Joan, me and my good friend and assistant from Home Interiors days, Bob Armstrong.

It was clear from the beginning that this company was to be "uniquely different." We were building the company on Biblical principles. Our Founding Verse was Proverbs 16:11: "The Lord demands fairness in every business deal. He established this principle" (TLB). This was not just some high-sounding religious platitude. It meant that we needed to act with honesty and integrity in the real world of business and not make promises we could not keep. The only thing we would promise was an *opportunity*. I remember laying all this out on a writing pad:

Our Founding Principle—To honor God and serve others!

Our Founding Philosophy—We believe that every person has worth and value because they are created by God in His image. We believe in America and the free enterprise system. We believe that it is more important to build a successful life than a successful business. We believe that real success comes when your priorities are in the right place and your life is in balance—God first, family second and business third.

Our Founding Purpose—To enrich every life we touch.

Our Founding Plan—To retail high fashion jewelry through Home Shows, because that is the best way to fulfill our Purpose and for our Jewelers to make money and to grow their businesses.

Also, from day one, our four reasons for starting Premier were clearly stated.

1. We wanted a company that would support

Christian ministries in America and around the world.

2. We wanted to offer an opportunity for mothers to be able to stay home more with their children.

3. We wanted to minister to single parents and provide a way in which they could be encouraged, increase their self-esteem, and do something worthwhile while supporting their children.

4. We wanted a company that could provide a way for individuals, especially those in full-time Christian work, to meet their financial needs. At the same time, we wanted to provide an oppor-tunity for wives of pastors and church staff members to find a ministry and identity of their own outside the church.

The more we got into the thinking and planning, the more excited we got. God was offering Joan and me an opportunity to help folks meet their financial needs and to support His work around the world. The potential was awesome, and we could hardly wait to see all that God would do.

From the beginning we made it clear that the principle of service needed to be fundamental in all our thinking and in all our organization. We wanted this to be a direct *service* company, not a direct sales company. Serving was going to be the heart of Premier Designs.

We held our first "Opportunity Presentation" in our home in December of 1985. Nita Barker, a friend and colleague from our Home Interiors days, signed up to become our very first "Jeweler," the name we gave our independent distributors. Bruce Peterson soon followed as a Jeweler, and not too many months later he began working with us to develop new markets. We were off and running. Within six months, we had 300 people, and by the end of 1986, we had over 700 Jewelers in 35 states. The sky was as blue as a hot August day in Texas. But just as suddenly, thunderclouds began to gather on the horizon.

"*Find something you love to do
and would do for nothing; then find
someone who will pay you to do it.*"

MARY CROWLEY

✤

"*People are always your road to success.
Love them enough to always expect their best.*"

ANDY HORNER

CHAPTER EIGHT

The Rebirth of Premier

We were off to a great start. Premier Designs was growing. Joan and I were certain we were doing what God wanted us to do. Our Philosophy and Purpose were well thought out and written down. But in a matter of months, it became clear that we had internal problems with our infant company. It had two completely different hearts, and it could not survive with this condition.

TIMES OF TESTING

From the beginning, everyone in leadership had agreed to the same Philosophy and Purpose, but reports from the office and the field began to make it clear that this agreement was in word only. Some from the Home Office were not practicing what was being preached. Things were being done that contradicted everything we stood for.

Close friends warned us about the difficulties and advised Joan and me to increase our involvement. We

91

had been overseeing the day-to-day operations, finances and accounting, but had deliberately stayed in the background as far as the field operations went. Our friends warned that if we didn't get involved there, our financial investment could be lost. More importantly, Premier would lose its integrity, and thus its reason for being.

We heeded their counsel. Joan began paying all bills and watching the inventory and receiving. I ran the office, set up auditing practices, and developed more policies and procedures. We got involved in planning our Rally and in some aspects of the training.

Even so, we continued to hear of things being said and promises being made that alarmed us. The emphasis was on making money, lots of it, and this emphasis contradicted everything we believed. The recruiting of new Jewelers was being placed ahead of serving others. "Book, sell, recruit"—and not necessarily in that order—was the motto. We were on the way to simply becoming another false-hope direct sales company more interested in profits than in people—exactly what Joan and I did not want.

Joan and I both remembered the exhaustion and hard work of going out into the field on a regular basis from our Home Interiors days, and in our sixties we hardly wanted to resume that pace again. But we also knew we must get to the field or the company's Purpose would evaporate. We boarded planes and met the people, working to get the message across. But at this point, I made a big mistake. I placed a man whom I trusted in the position of president. On the outside he went along with me, but inside he had very different core values and beliefs about direct sales and about the future of Premier Designs. His values and my values contradicted one another. I kept thinking that I could bring him around to our way of doing things. In the meantime, not many people realized that the company belonged to us or that the Horners were in control.

These early years were not only about power struggles and difficulties; there were also many blessings. Joan and I continued to make mission trips, many with Bruce and Maggie Peterson, who shared our heart for missions. We got involved with an orphanage in Portugal and with Ireland Outreach. We extended our involvements through Word of Life ministries in Argentina, Bolivia, Brazil, Chile, Ecuador, Mexico, Paraguay, Poland and Venezuela. God was opening our eyes to more and more needs, and the outreach of the company expanded. What a thrill to see God's plan unfold even though the developing storm in our office did not dissipate.

Peace in the Midst of Turmoil

Rushing through O'Hare airport in Chicago, I felt sharp chest pains. I had been noticing a growing fatigue, too—a kind of weariness and tiredness I hadn't experienced before. *I must be getting old*, I thought. *Can't keep up the pace I used to!* I wasn't sure what these symptoms meant, but I decided to check things out. My cardiologist confirmed that I had some problems: three arteries were seriously blocked. He thought they could "roto rooter" the obstructions and I would be as good as new.

In November 1989, I underwent angioplasty surgery. It went well, and as I lay in the recovery room, a deep peace and a quiet joy came over me that I have never experienced before in my life. When I came out of that hospital, I emerged with a clear purpose. I would proclaim the truth regardless of what people thought. I would tell others what I believed and explain why God ordained this company. I would invest time in our leadership and make sure they "caught" the vision in their hearts, not just in their heads or with their mouths. Our company had been created to serve and to give hope to everyone we touched. We existed to influence the homes of America with service, hope and joy. By God's grace and strength, this was going to become a reality.

As I recovered from surgery, I drafted my ideas in a document titled "Pathway Through the '90s." I clearly set forth why the company was founded and what I envisioned for its future. I sketched out the creation of a Premier Foundation, which eventually would own part of the company and see to it that profits were distributed among various ministry and charitable endeavors. I made it crystal clear that no one person would ever have ownership or control of Premier. I wasn't fooling around any more with any mixed purposes or ego trips.

This written clarification set in motion a coup within the ranks. I had tried for over two years to conquer the divisiveness and conflict, to work with everyone, to give them time to come around. I had hoped that eventually we would be of one mind. That was not to be.

In response to the clear parameters of the "Pathway Through the '90s" document, the president at the time secretly set up his own direct sales jewelry company in May 1990 and began to recruit our Jewelers. Rumors flew and things were said about us and about Premier that were absolutely untrue. People were told that Premier was going out of business, so they should jump ship while they could. Offers were made to our best people in an attempt to get them to leave and bring their down lines—the people they had sponsored into the business—with them. Joan and I were harassed, lied about and called names, and this hurt us deeply. Even worse, people we cared about were being hurt, and that crushed us. By the time it was all over, nearly half our Jewelers went with them. It was a huge blow.

We consulted our attorneys, and our case was crystal clear. Our president and his wife had completely violated their contracts by starting a new company down the street while still working for Premier. My lawyers wanted to fight: "Go get them, Andy! You have a solid case. We can destroy them!" My managers and Field Leadership counseled war: "You can't let them get away with this, Andy. They can't be allowed to do this!" We started to prepare our legal case against them.

THE MIRACLE OF AN IRISHMAN'S SILENCE

I am an Irishman, and I know the power of words and can use them. When I face a crisis, my first response is to talk and to come on strong. But in this case, something unusual happened to me that had never happened before in my life.

The night after planning our case with our lawyers, I went to sleep and had one of those vivid dreams. In the dream, I was in Jerusalem standing with a group of people. We were watching a man up front who was on trial. There was a sign above his head that read, "The King of the Jews." I spotted his accusers, and I listened as they hurled one accusation after another at Jesus, but He never said a word. He just stood there. They increased their yelling and the power of their cursing, but Jesus continued to simply stand there in silence. When I woke up, it hit me. There is power in silence.

I called our lawyers and said, "Forget it. We are dropping our battle plan. We are not going to do a thing." I called our key leaders in the field, the women and men who stood with us and who strongly wanted to go to war for Premier. "We are not going to say a word about this situation," I told them. My friends couldn't believe what I was saying. "We are not going to say anything negative about those who have betrayed us or attack their new company," I said. "In fact, I want us to be completely silent. We are not going to sue them. Instead, we will simply start again and get busy rebuilding. We will not take legal action against them."

Elizabeth and Randy Draper and Melissa and Greg Terrell went through this time of crisis with Joan and me. They heard my strange directive to keep quiet and not fight. Let me have them each share in their own words their reaction to the split that occurred in 1990.

ৠ

Elizabeth and Randy Draper *have attained the strategic position of Diamond Executive Directors, the highest position that can be earned in our field organization. They live in the Dallas area and have worked their business faithfully for over twenty years with great integrity. They have received many awards: the Tom Hemingway Excellence in Leadership award, the Marge Caldwell Encourager of the Year award, and the Twenty Years of Special Service award. Both have been recognized individually for their character with our most prestigious awards: Elizabeth was named Premier Princess in 1989, and Randy was named Mr. Premier in 2007. Here is Randy's story:*

My wife, Elizabeth, and I were home one evening when the phone rang. It was Andy. We loved getting calls from Andy and Joan. They weren't that involved in the Field Marketing side of the business in those days. Instead, they primarily threw themselves into the operations of the company. They were always so upbeat and positive. Their encouragement went a long way with Elizabeth and me. We had lost $750,000 in our building business during the real estate crash in Texas, and were going through some tough financial times. Our Premier business was our only source of income. We desperately needed every dollar we could make just to keep our heads above water.

Andy asked how our two boys were doing, and how Elizabeth was. Then he said, "I have some good news and some bad news." I said, "What's the good news?" He replied that he had fired the president and his wife that afternoon. I thought, *Wow, if this is the good news, I can't wait to hear the bad news!* I asked him what had happened, and he began to tell me how he had discovered that they were starting a new direct sales jewelry company on the side.

I wasn't totally shocked at the news. Six months earlier, Andy had shared with the leadership that he was going to set up a foundation, and that all Premier Designs' stock would be left in this non-profit foundation for the purpose of supporting missions. The president had not been happy about this concept. Still, I couldn't believe what I was hearing. In the early days of our Premier business, the president had mentored me, challenged me and encouraged me. He taught me how to present the marketing plan and how to build our business. Elizabeth and I had trusted him. Now he was stealing my organization and my income. When I heard the news, I felt personally betrayed. It seemed like a bad dream.

Andy then went on to tell me that about 500 of our most active Jewelers were going to leave Premier and go with the new company. (When the dust cleared later, Elizabeth and I ended up losing 90 people.) Andy finished the call with some encouraging words, and we agreed to stay in touch over the next few days. I immediately called some close friends in Premier, and we began to plan our strategy. Were we ever fired up! We would call all the people who were leaving. We were angry at the rumors we were hearing about the Horners and the future of Premier Designs. We were going to do whatever it took to get even. We were going to let people know the truth.

Then, Andy called again. I couldn't believe it when he told us what the Lord had put on his heart. We were not to say anything to any of the former Jewelers or Leaders. God had impressed upon him to remain silent. I was shocked. I told him that we could put these guys out of business for what they had done. We couldn't let them get away with this!

Andy replied, "I know we have a great case. I know that we can do something legally about it, but I know God wants us to let it rest and leave it in His hands. I am confident that things will work out as they should." Many of you know that I am not your quiet type. Reluctantly, I agreed to do as Andy asked.

Our National Rallies were a few weeks away, and Andy asked if we would fly with them to Charlotte, North Carolina, and Houston, Texas. On the flight we talked about what was going on. Andy shared with me the peace he had. He asked me to speak to the people at both Rallies to reassure them and let them know that everything was going to be okay.

I checked into the hotel in Charlotte and went to my room with a heavy heart. How could I tell people that everything was going to be okay when I did not know the future and did not have that peace myself? I went to sleep that night with a troubled spirit. I always get nervous before I speak, but this was different. There would be people in the audience the next day who had already decided to go with the other company. There would be people in that audience who were planning to stay in Premier and who had put an awful lot of faith in us and in this company. I could not sleep. I tossed and turned all night.

Finally, I got up about 5:30 a.m. and grabbed my Bible. I put my fingers together and said, "God, I need a promise." I opened the Bible and scanned the pages for an answer. It wasn't there. I closed the Bible and tried one more time. This time I opened the Bible to the book of Haggai. I didn't even know Haggai was in the Bible. I thought Haggai was the old woman that Brutus was always trying to fix up with Popeye. But I began reading in the second chapter of Haggai. When I read Scripture, I always personalize it by inserting my name and my situation. Here is what I read that morning:

"In the seventh month (*interesting—it was July 1990*), the word of the LORD came by Haggai the prophet saying, 'Speak now (*to Randy*) . . . and to the remnant of the people saying, "Who is left among you who saw this temple (*company*) in its former glory? And how do you see it now? *(I honestly didn't know how we were going to make it without the Jewelers we had lost.)* . . . But now take courage *(Randy)*, . . . and all you people of the land take courage . . . and work; for I am with you," declares the LORD of hosts. . . . "My Spirit is abiding in your midst; do not fear! *(That was such a comfort to me because I had always felt that Premier was God's company and that His Spirit was in our midst.)* . . . I will fill this house with glory," says the LORD of hosts. "The silver is Mine and the gold is Mine. *(Yeah, He's in the jewelry business!)* . . . The latter glory of this house will be greater than the former, . . . and in this place I shall give peace," declares the LORD of hosts.' " (Haggai 2:1-9, NASB).

When I went out that morning to talk to the Jewelers about our future, I didn't need to tell them that Andy and Joan had told me everything was going to be okay. I was able to tell them with confidence that everything was going to be okay because God had given *me* a promise!

Over the years, I have often reviewed that passage and been reminded of the goodness of God. He came to me when I was nervous and distressed. He gave me a promise that has been lived out in front of my eyes. The latter glory of Premier Designs is definitely greater than the former. We have continued to grow and have been able to enrich the lives of countless thousands of people each year. Our company survived, and it was definitely by God's design and guidance.

❧

Melissa and Greg Terrell have attained the position of Diamond Executive Directors. They live in the Houston area and have worked in Premier for over twenty years. Their faithful service has not gone unnoticed. They received the Tom Hemingway Excellence in Leadership award in 2005, Melissa was named the 1994 Premier Princess, and Greg was our 2007 Mr. Premier. Here is their story of what happened:

In 1990, Andy and Joan took the Four Diamond Designers (the top leadership in the company at that time) to Rhode Island to visit the manufacturing facilities that were producing Premier Designs' jewelry. It was an awesome trip, seeing firsthand how the jewelry was made.

While we were there, Andy shared his vision for the next decade and talked about how the main focus of Premier Designs' "Pathway Through the '90s" would be to support ministries. He shared what could happen as our company remained true to our founding Philosophy and Purpose, which was to honor God and serve people. He told us that a foundation with a board of trustees would be established in order to secure this plan.

After the meeting was over, Melissa and I met with my parents, Beverly and Jack Terrell, along with Elizabeth and Randy Draper. We were all excited about what the Horners wanted to do with Premier. We clearly saw incredible God-given wisdom in this plan for the future. However, the other three Four Diamond couples, as well as Premier's president and his wife, were less enthusiastic. We soon found out the reason why. Earlier that year, a group within Premier Designs had started putting together another jewelry company. Looking back, we can clearly see that our company had been divided.

Later, while we were on a trip to Hawaii in July of 1990, my parents called and told us that the company had "split." Initially, we were struck with fear, uncertain of the future. We couldn't help but wonder if Premier Designs would still be there when we got back to Texas. When we returned, Andy and Joan reassured us. They reminded us that Premier was God's company and that we were all in His hands. They kept trusting God and helped us to trust Him, too. Our down line people were calling us, nervously asking what was going to happen to Premier. We told them to stick with Joan and Andy. We could trust them. I had known the Horners since I was a little kid. We had gone to the same church. I never had to wonder, "Can I trust Premier" or "Can I trust the Horners?" When Andy and Joan said it would be okay, I knew it would be okay.

Our Regional Rally that summer was scheduled in the midst of a very confusing time at Premier Designs. The Horners were being accused of not knowing how to run a company; lies were being told about their character. These accusations were unbelievable and ridiculous. We couldn't wait for the Horners to get to the Houston Rally, so we could show them our love and support. It was a day we will always remember. Their humble hearts had been so broken by the personal attacks, but God used our enthusiastic and loving people to restore their vision and belief that God's ways are bigger than our ways.

That fall season of 1990 was an incredible ordeal. The Home Office thought that the jewelry inventory had been ordered. However, as Home Show orders arrived, they quickly found out they did not have all the jewelry. Home Office Associates, including Andy and Joan, worked tirelessly to find pieces of jewelry to fulfill Home Show orders by Christmas Day. When the Horners realized that many customers would not receive their jewelry by Christmas, they offered to give each customer free jewelry, worth $25 retail, for each piece of jewelry that did not arrive by Christmas Day. Wow! Customers were so impressed that many of them were hoping their jewelry would *not* arrive so they would receive the free jewelry. This selfless, generous act of service won over a lot of customers and Jewelers. It showed that Premier Designs really did care.

Yes, it was a difficult year. Many of the people who left told us that Premier was going to fold; that the Horners didn't know anything about jewelry, etc. The Jewelers who left to go with the other company were looking for greener pastures, but they didn't find them. We have now been with Premier for more than twenty years. Melissa and I have grown to love, respect and trust the Horners more with each passing year. They have kept Premier on the right course since its inception, and we can all trust that Premier Designs will continue to stay on course in the years to come.

❧

PREMIER: PHASE TWO

Despite the deep pain of that year, Joan and I can now look back and say that it was good. It was a time of needed purging. Our vision for Premier was purified and clarified. We recommitted ourselves to enriching lives, ministering to others, and serving. Those who weathered the storm with us were the cream of the crop, and we will always be grateful for their loyalty, support and love during those difficult months. They were the ones who believed what we believed and had the same vision for Premier as we did. We were fewer in number, but we were stronger and more vital because everyone now had the same purpose. I always said that I would rather have ten people with heart and commitment than a thousand without it, and I believed that then more than ever.

Essentially, we had a brand-new company and a brand-new start. We had a strong foundation of committed people, and it was time to build. Joan and I spent the next several years on the road, encouraging our people, and communicating over and over again why Premier exists and what it is all about. We had never intended to be so involved or so busy when we started the company, but God had other plans, and as we obeyed, He blessed.

As I look back on that time, I remember it as some of the most difficult years of our lives. At one point, I seriously thought about quitting. But then I remembered this wasn't my plan; it was God's plan, so I could let Him take care of it. And He has. We wouldn't have chosen the pain and suffering that the split caused. But we are grateful that God kept us on track, and also showed us that sometimes silence is golden.

These are the facts and the history of the birth of Premier. But what about the inner workings? What is the heart of Premier and what are the principles that continue to guide it? Why is Premier a company people trust? Let's look at what makes this company tick.

PART TWO

The Heart

of

Premier

"It is important how you view your business.
If you look at serving, instead of selling,
you will be richly rewarded."

ANDY HORNER

※

"Forget about the sales you hope to make.
Concentrate on the service you want to render."

HARRY BULLIS
FORMER CHAIRMAN OF GENERAL MILLS

CHAPTER NINE

The Inverted Pyramid

he black stretch limousine pulls up to the curb in New York City. The windows are tinted, and everything about the car whispers wealth and power. The chauffeur rushes to open the door for his passenger. As Donald Trump strides into his Trump Towers, a battery of secretaries, managers and personal aides jumps to meet his every need. This is the epitome of business success—to reach the apex of the pyramid, the top, where everyone now serves you.

In 3000 B.C. the Pharaohs mobilized an entire nation to build the pyramids to ensure that their names would be remembered forever. Today, the Pharaohs of modern business build their skyscrapers and mobilize their armies of employees to meet their ego needs. Having others wait on you hand and foot— isn't this what being at the top is all about?

TOP-DOWN PYRAMID

The organizational diagram of a hierarchical, top-down corporation would look something like this:

This type of organization is typical of today's corporations. The customers provide the foundation of the entire structure, supporting each of the subsequent levels. Employees are there to support the managers and all those above them, and managers are there to support the CEO and his executives. Those at the very top of the company don't have to worry about supporting anyone. They have reached the zenith of power where they can do what they want, as long as they make sure that the company keeps making money.

THE PYRAMID TURNED UPSIDE DOWN

In contrast to most business tycoons who don Armani suits and monogrammed silk shirts, the most powerful man who ever lived took off His robe, wrapped a towel around His waist and proceeded to wash the filthy, smelly feet of His disciples. He taught us that true success is not climbing up, but bowing down to meet the needs of others. He said, "The first shall be last and the last shall be first."

Following His example, we do things a little differently at Premier Designs. Our organizational chart is upside down when compared to most. I call it the "Inverted Pyramid." It was never taught to me in college, nor had I ever heard of it in my years of corporate experience.

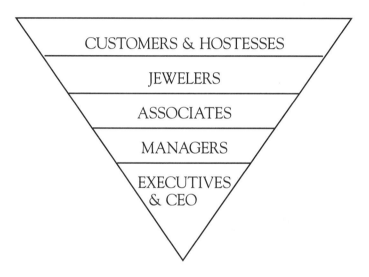

As you can see, the difference between this pyramid and the more typical top-down pyramid on the previous page is that the "higher" you go in this upside-down organizational structure, the more people you are responsible to support and serve. Those who purchase the jewelry (the customers) and those who provide a home in which the Jewelers present the jewelry (the Hostesses) are at the top of the pyramid. The people who sell the jewelry (Jewelers), Associates and other Managers follow. Those in "higher" positions don't have more people serving them; they have more people to serve. This demonstrates what I believe is a fundamental truth: *Leading is serving and serving is leading.* Advancement means greater responsibility in meeting the needs of others; it means becoming a servant. Do you want to move up the ladder? Learn to support others and meet their needs. Want a title and more responsibility? Become a better servant.

Looking at our pyramid, you might say, "That's top heavy. It looks like it could topple over any minute, with just the slightest nudge." It won't. It is held firmly in position by four strong pillars: our Philosophy, our Purpose, our Plan, and our Service.

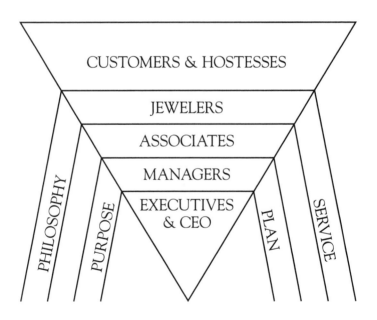

Our Philosophy

We believe that every person has worth and value because they are created by God and in His image. Mary Crowley repeatedly reminded me, "God did not take time to make a nobody." We believe that God created every person with value and that every person deserves our respect. We believe that people are important not because of what they achieve, but because of who they are. We believe that people are our most important asset.

We believe in America and the free enterprise system. We love this country and the freedom and opportunity we have to achieve in direct proportion to our willingness to work.

We believe that it is more important to build a successful life than a successful business. Real success comes when your priorities are in the right place and your life is in balance: *God first, family second, work third.*

Our Purpose

We clearly stated our Purpose in November 1985 when we began Premier, and it is still the same: *To Enrich Every Life We Touch.* This means that we must *serve, share* and *care,* striving to add something positive to each life that we come in contact with. As a company, enriching lives means *providing a way for those who join the Premier Family to find identity, achievement and success, and to meet their personal and financial needs.* Everyone whom God has created has the basic need to feel that they are valued, that they belong, and that they are competent. As a company, Premier reassures people of their worth and value. It provides a family for them to belong to and helps them succeed in their business.

OUR PLAN

Retailing through Home Shows is our Plan, and we have an excellent Hostess Plan (we believe one of the best you will find anywhere) that motivates and generously rewards the Hostess for holding a Home Show. We could sell our jewelry through stores, catalogs, a shopping channel or even the Internet, but our experience has shown that Home Shows are the most effective means.

First of all, Home Shows are the best way to fulfill our purpose of enriching lives. They allow us into the homes of America to bring a dose of hope. Because they provide an opportunity to build long-term relationships and give personalized service to Hostesses and customers, Home Shows allow Jewelers to demonstrate their caring and to practice what we preach.

Additionally, Home Shows are the most direct way for our Jewelers to grow their businesses and achieve immediate financial rewards. Jewelers receive their profit as soon as they make the sale, that very night, resulting in immediate income. Moreover, building relationships with Hostesses and customers through Home Shows creates a retail base and a pool of people who will be repeat Hostesses and customers. We have some Hostesses who not only become their Jeweler's friend, but also enthusiastically hold four or five Shows a year. And if the Jeweler is interested in building a sales organization, experience has shown that she will find her best sponsoring contacts at Home Shows.

SERVICE

Serving others is the heart of Premier. I cannot emphasize this enough. The company is saturated with a focus on service. When you call our Home Office, the phone is answered, "How may I serve you?" We talk about service constantly, train on it, write about it, and even paint it on our walls. We have it on our letterhead: "Serving with care since 1985." Jewelers are trained to serve customers; our Home Office Associates (employees) are trained to serve and support our Jewelers; and we all try to serve and help one another in whatever ways we can. All of our people understand that service is the road to success. Everything we do relates to service.

All this talk about service could sound insincere and unrealistic, and we certainly are not perfect at it, but let me assure you that this is not just talk. Serving others is not just a slogan or some program we do halfheartedly. We mean it. If you come by our Home Office, I believe you will feel it. You will sense a difference because this attitude of serving is deep in the heart of our Associates. We work diligently and tirelessly to create and maintain this service atmosphere at our Home Office and to communicate this attitude to everyone who comes into the Premier Family.

We do the same with our Jewelers in the field. As Joan and I travel the country, meeting and talking with our Jewelers, we constantly talk about service.

Over and over, we repeat our message that serving others is the road to success and fulfillment. We say it again and again, and then we say it some more because we want people to get this from their heads into their hearts. We want them to understand that true service is an attitude that sincerely asks of every situation, "How can I turn this into an opportunity to serve?"

For example, we sell jewelry, the number one gift item in America. Jewelry is a great product and we are very proud of our line, but it is also a delicate, vulnerable product. Jewelry can break, stones can fall out, and finishes can tarnish. Because of these problems, it can be a frustrating product at times. What I want our Jewelers to see is that these problems are, in fact, opportunities to serve. Instead of looking at these situations as time-wasters and impediments to their businesses, those with true serving hearts will see these situations as exciting opportunities to serve their customers and go out of their way to help, expecting nothing back.

A Lesson from Napoleon

In my house I have a small collection of Napoleon ceramics. Why? It is said of Napoleon that he was a gifted man, a visionary and a dreamer of dreams. His leadership in war was excelled by none. When he overthrew the royalty, he had good intentions. He wanted to help and improve the living conditions in the lives of the common people. Considered a brilliant leader, Napoleon is remembered for quotes such as, "Courage is like love. It must have hope for nourishment," and "I would rather have one lion lead a hundred antelopes than a hundred antelopes lead one lion." He understood the meaning of leadership and had great success, as history reveals.

But Napoleon was unable to handle his successes and wanted more. Conquering most of Europe was not enough. He wanted to conquer the world. As he lost his original purpose, selfishness, recognition and power corrupted him. He was a dynamic young man, but ended up an old man in despair, a prisoner on the isle of Corsica. I have a picture of Napoleon in his early days, young and handsome. And I have a picture of him in his later days, an old man, hopeless and broken.

Years have passed and times have changed since the days of Napoleon. However, human nature has not changed. People start out with a purpose to help and serve others. But often when they receive recognition, they are corrupted by power and decide enough is never enough. The grace with which a leader handles success has a tremendous influence on others. As Albert Schweitzer said, "Example is not the main thing in influencing others, it is the only thing." This is why it is so important that the leaders of a company maintain the desire and ability to serve others, even as the company reaches greater success.

All of this idealistic emphasis on service and caring for others will mean nothing if it is not combined with solid management principles. I've had decades of hands-on experience in the world of big business and in direct sales. Let me share some of the practical principles I have gleaned from this experience.

*"For the Lord grants wisdom! His every word is a
treasure of knowledge and understanding....
He shows how to distinguish right from wrong,
how to find the right decision every time."*

Proverbs 2:6, 9, TLB

*"After a company is established, service
and support are the keys to success."*

Andy Horner

CHAPTER TEN

Management Principles

t Premier Designs, we operate with skilled Managers who utilize proven management practices. This is a well-run company, and our operations and accounting practices stand up to the toughest scrutiny. I brought to Premier almost twenty years of experience in corporate America and eighteen years of experience in direct selling. From these years of work, I gleaned a set of business principles and management activities that have guided Premier from the beginning. They make us *uniquely different* from any other direct selling company that I know of.

These distinctive principles are significant for two reasons. First, *they work.* Premier is a successful and growing company that continues to demonstrate the truth and power of these principles. Second, I want to dispel the notion that there is some inherent contradiction between building a company on Biblical principles and managing a company with sound financial and business principles. In my mind, they are one and the same thing.

It's easy for a business person to put on his or her fancy clothes on Sunday morning and sing the hymns with gusto. It's another thing to bring God into the Monday-morning world of buying and selling. I believe honoring God gets down to the basics. It means you are truthful, honest and financially responsible. It means you never make promises you cannot keep. It means you use the mind God gave you. Solid business principles, whether you claim to be a Christian or not, are essential to building a solid company. We pay the consequences in life and in business for foolish decisions and mismanagement.

PRINCIPLE #1: PUT PEOPLE FIRST

I firmly believe that people are the most important asset any company has. This means *people come first at Premier*. We focus on people—our customers, our Hostesses, our Jewelers and our Home Office Associates—rather than on profit, production or product. Remember our emphasis on serving? This means that meeting the needs of people is a higher priority than selling jewelry.

I prefer to call Premier a *direct service* company, rather than a direct sales company. I make this distinction because there is a difference between a company that emphasizes sales, production and the bottom line, and a company that puts people first, supporting them and serving them, expecting nothing in return. Our Jewelers are never asked, "How were your sales this month?" We have no required weekly reports and no quotas. We believe and train that success comes in serving others and seeing lives changed, not in selling jewelry. Our focus is people.

Although Premier is primarily about people and not profits, this does not mean that there isn't opportunity to make a good profit. We have seen time and time again that *you can sell without serving, but you cannot serve without selling.* Most people sign up to make money, and many do very well. We want them to do well. We offer one of the best money-making opportunities available. However, we also want them to think beyond the money to serving people.

PEOPLE FIRST IN THE FIELD

Joan and I decided when we started Premier that our focus was not going to be on making big money for the company or enriching ourselves financially. The company would have to make enough of a profit to stay in business, of course, but beyond that, we wanted the people who do the work to make the money. Mary Crowley taught us well. "Andy," she would say, "you find enough people to care about, and *you help them succeed*, and you can't help but succeed yourself."

We knew the wisdom of her words and put them into practice. We instituted a higher than normal payout on sales—50 percent—almost unheard of in the direct sales industry, along with a very generous commission structure of 10 percent three levels down, plus extra percentages for moving up in our Diamond Designer Leadership program. We certainly could have structured this differently and less generously, but we knew that if we meant what we said—that people were first—this meant that they must be first in the payout. Their earnings needed to be generous enough that doing Home Shows and building a business was well worth their time and efforts and would provide them an opportunity for financial success in direct proportion to the time and work that they invested.

In addition to providing the opportunity for good incomes, we wanted to do everything we could to help the Jewelers succeed at their businesses. To this day, we keep our jewelry prices as low as possible so Jewelers can sell it more easily, even if it means our profit margins are smaller. We mark up our business supplies and catalogs very little, if any, so a Jeweler's cost of doing business stays as low as possible. We pay for all shipping and postage, even though those costs routinely exceed the small annual licensing fee the Jewelers pay. We do no advertising. Instead, we put the money back into the Jewelers' businesses with promotions, contests, incentives and subsidies—all aimed at helping the Jeweler succeed. In other words, *we put our money where our Jewelers are.*

Not only does the principle of *people first* guide our financial decisions, it also influences our thinking when we develop policies and procedures. Joan and I felt that putting our people first meant that we should go the extra mile for them in terms of our Home Office support and service. We determined to do everything we could to make their businesses as hassle-free as possible.

For example, we fill orders by customer and by Home Show, and then package them accordingly so that the Jeweler has no unpacking, dividing up and repackaging to do. We didn't want them receiving large boxes of merchandise for several Home Shows at a time, requiring them to spend a lot of time processing their customer orders. Moreover, we file sales taxes for our Jewelers in all fifty states and Puerto Rico. We provide monthly commission reports for each Jeweler. All this is included in the reasonable annual renewal fee and keeps the business as simple as possible. Although these services translate into higher operating costs for the Home Office and Distribution Center, they give our Jewelers more time to focus on people, which is where we want their focus to be.

Our focus on people extends to our programs of awards and recognitions as well. It is typical in direct sales companies that those who achieve and sell the most are the ones who are recognized and honored, and they should be. We recognize our top performers with awards and prizes, pins, certificates and onstage presentations at our Rallies. However, we also want to honor those who do work hard but who, because of circumstances or personality or timing, will never be top achievers. We want ways to recognize people for who they are, not just what they do.

So, over the years we have inaugurated a number of awards for those who embody the heart and vision of Premier, the caring and sharing Principles that guide us. For example, our top two awards are our "Premier Princess" and "Mr. Premier." These awards are not based on production or sponsoring. Instead, they are given to a lady and a man who have demonstrated a serving heart and a sharing and caring spirit. Caring, sharing and serving are the most important things to us. In 2001, we gave out our first Tom Hemingway Excellence in Leadership award, which is presented to a Jeweler or couple who have demonstrated excellence in leadership by living a life of honesty and integrity and have a desire to help others succeed. That same year we honored our first recipient of the Vision award to a lady who was able to look at the year ahead and visualize the needs of her people, and then set out to motivate them to succeed. We have a Spirit of Service award that is presented to the Jeweler who has faithfully worked her business and dedicated many years of service to Premier. Our newest award is the Marge Caldwell Encourager of the Year award, which is presented to a Jeweler or couple who uplift and encourage others. At our Home Office and Distribution Center, we have many walls dedicated to the recipients because we greatly appreciate them. At Premier, these awards for "who you are" are the highest awards you can receive.

PEOPLE FIRST IN THE HOME OFFICE

Most of the examples I have given relate to ways that we put people first out in the field. However, our policies and practices in the Home Office also focus on people. We realize the essential contribution that everyone in the Home Office makes to the success of our company. Every job that is done is important, and every person makes a valuable contribution. We take every opportunity we can to express our appreciation, both in words and in actions. In fact, we decided that the term *employee* didn't really reflect the reality of our company. Rather, we are "Associates," all working together in an enterprise we believe in. Without our Associates, we wouldn't be where we are today.

Focusing on people in the Home Office means that we want our Associates to receive fair wages and to share the profits of the company. We take care of our Associates before we do anything else. We have profit-sharing programs, 401(k)s, a generous benefit package, a loan program, a school reimbursement plan, and a scholarship program for college students. We select Associates of the Year, recognizing them for their competence, but mainly for their attitude of serving others. At our July Rally, we bring many of our Associates up on stage to *publicly* thank them for all they do to serve our Jewelers. At that time, we announce the recipient of our Servant's Heart award, which recognizes that individual within our organization, in the Home Office and Distribution Center, who best exemplifies the Premier Spirit of Service. We host several parties throughout the year, including our annual Christmas party where we give bonuses, gifts, prizes and cash. And my door is never shut. I am available and eager to meet with any of our people who need or want to talk. They come first.

The principle of putting people first at the Home Office even influenced the decision about the location of our new corporate headquarters. When we decided to buy our new building in 1992, there were many buildings for sale in the Dallas area. We could have done better price-wise and helped out our bottom line if we had moved farther east than we did. However, most of our people live west of our office. Joan and I decided that if our people truly come first, they should be a more important factor in where we located the company than the financial implications. We bought west.

I imagine that some of you think we must be nuts to make decisions this way. But I want to tell you that there is power in this principle of putting people first. Sure, it may have reduced our profits somewhat, but I believe that you never give without getting even more back. How do you measure in dollars the value of employee loyalty, happiness in their jobs and with their workplace, high morale, and the extra efforts that are made because they know they are truly cared about and appreciated? I remember Mary Crowley's coaching, "Andy, you build the people and the people will build the business." She was right.

PEOPLE FIRST WITH OUR SUPPLIERS

Our principle of putting people first also extends to our suppliers and vendors. We are grateful for their products and services. We need the boxes and paper, the equipment and phone lines, and good, quality jewelry. One of the first things Joan and I did in 1990, after the company's realignment, was to visit our jewelry suppliers in Rhode Island. We deliberately went to see each one at their plants. We wanted to get to know them personally and see their businesses and how they operated. It was a valuable time of bridge building, and we developed relationships that we treasure to this day.

In 1993, we gave an appreciation dinner for our Rhode Island suppliers. We thanked them for their good service, told them about our business philosophy, and let them know that we considered them a vital part of our Premier team. These folks meant more to us than just a source of product. What a strange experience for these battle-hardened business people! They weren't used to being cared about personally. They were used to being manipulated and pitted against one another. Their enthusiastic response became one more proof of the importance of our first and foremost principle of doing business—focus on people.

The Personal Touch

We believe that putting people first also requires a personal touch. When you call Premier, a person will answer the phone. We do not have automated answering that presents some complicated menu in order for you to direct your call. Automated answering and voice mail are absolutely forbidden! We have real live operators, an anachronism in this day and age. It is people to people, not people to machine or system. It would be a lot cheaper to have automated answering—paying three or four operators to answer phones and direct calls is expensive—but I believe personal service is vital if we are to be a company whose central focus is truly people. We cannot lose that personal touch.

Now don't get me wrong. Technology can be good, and we use every bit available to help us do a better job of serving people. We use very sophisticated hardware and software systems for order processing, inventory control, accounting and shipping. We are committed to staying informed of all new developments and upgrading as we need to, even though sometimes it seems we are upgrading daily! But our computers and systems do not dictate what we do. They are tools to be used to better serve our people, but never, never, never are they substitutes for a person!

Sometimes maintaining a personal touch takes extra effort, but it is always worth it. It lets people know how much you care about them and appreciate them. Joan and I write personal notes to our folks in the field and in the Home Office and Distribution Center. Joan even hand writes every one of hers. We stay in touch, person-to-person, and it means so much. I personally sign all achievement certificates as our people reach new levels in their businesses. This takes two or three days out of my month, but I wouldn't do it any other way. For me, focusing on people means that our contacts with people must be this personal. People will always come first at Premier.

PRINCIPLE #2: CONTROL THE GROWTH

Over the years, I have seen too many direct sales companies grow faster than they were able to support and collapse in on themselves. When the demands of the field outrun the ability of the Home Office to supply and serve, the company is dead.

We decided that in order to avoid these problems we would deliberately control our growth. We wanted

Premier to grow very slowly and carefully. We were not interested in big numbers. Instead, we would invest in a smaller number of people. We would train them and help them really work their businesses. If they followed the Home Show Plan, with an emphasis on retailing rather than recruiting, we knew that both they and the company would be building on strong foundations.

Controlling growth also meant that we would not finance Premier's expanding operations by going into debt. We determined that the company would grow at a rate that it could sustain financially by itself, not with borrowed money. Although we realized that the day might come when some debt was necessary, we did not want to go out on any financial limbs simply for the purpose of getting big.

If we wanted to get big fast, we certainly could. We know how to do it. You simply require a very small investment to get started and offer incentives for joining that are too good to refuse. Then you watch the numbers grow. Getting big is not difficult, but it can be a problem.

In May 1995, we celebrated Joan's birthday with twelve days of special Home Show bonuses and incentives given to new Jewelers who signed up. Within a day or two, we were swamped with orders and new contracts. Within three days we were a week behind; within five days we were two weeks behind, and by the end of the contest, we had things so piled up we were three to four weeks behind. Things were out of control quickly, and there was much frustration and unhappiness in the field. Customers waited two or three weeks to get orders that are usually filled in three days. All this was a vivid reminder: control the growth! Premier is not about getting big; it is about enriching lives and serving others. It is about being sure we can adequately train, serve and support the Jewelers who sign on.

Tight control of finances is as important as tight control of growth. We are conservative in all of our financial operations. Since day one, we have taken extra efforts never to commingle monies. We never spend the money we collect for sales taxes. That money goes directly into an escrow account and is kept completely separate from our operating capital. We never spend commission money. The earned commissions are put aside in escrow until the commission checks are issued.

In addition, beginning in our first year of operation, we have had outside auditors come in annually to check everything over. We never want anything done that is not completely in line with standard accounting practices, the law and business ethics. We are proud to be members of the Direct Selling Association (DSA), an organization made up of direct selling companies who have been carefully checked out over a one-year period and who meet the high ethical and legal standards of the group. There are many wonderful direct selling companies who are members, and we are happy to be associated with them. Likewise, we applaud and support the efforts of the DSA in rooting out noncompliant and unethical direct sales companies and raising the standards of the industry as a whole.

We have committed ourselves to slow, controlled growth for two reasons. My eighteen years of experience in direct sales before starting Premier taught me an important lesson. The number that really counts in a direct sales company is not the number of people under contract, but rather the number of people who are actively working. It only makes sense. Who cares if you have millions of people signed up to sell your product if no one does it? Our goal, instead, has been and will continue to be to sign up people who want to work—individuals who want to enrich lives. We are looking for people who care and who want to serve.

The second powerful reason for controlling our growth is that slow, steady growth gives us time to develop strong leadership both in the field and in the Home Office—leaders who share our vision and our values. A company that grows faster than its leadership base can easily lose its way. It takes time for leaders to internalize the Founding Principles of our company. It takes time for them to learn how to live out our core values in the reality of their daily business lives. We are dedicated to training and developing this kind of committed leadership because it is the key to practicing what we preach. Authentic leadership must be in place if we are to sustain meaningful and lasting growth.

In summary, we are conservative, risk aversive, and debt avoidant in our financial operations. We pay all our vendors promptly and have never been even a day late with paychecks and commission checks. Our growth is slow and controlled, so that we can provide the service and support to the field that are essential to sustain the company over the long term. We do not grow any faster than we can serve. The principle of controlled growth and responsible finances permeates everything we do in the Home Office and out in the field. This is one message I preach loud and clear!

PRINCIPLE #3: COMMIT TO A SHARED VISION

When I began to think about starting a direct sales company at the age of sixty, I had a clear vision of what kind of company I wanted it to be: a company where serving and caring were the objectives above all others. This is the vision that motivates and inspires Joan and me and most of those who join Premier Designs. People need to make money, and they can in Premier, but what our people get the most excited about and motivated by is this added dimension of their business: that their work has meaning and purpose beyond just the money.

Communicating this vision for Premier with all who join us is a major part of my role at Premier. I feel it is my responsibility to keep these guiding Principles in front of our Associates and Jewelers alike. I want our Associates to understand the scope of what they do. They are not just inspecting a piece of jewelry; they also are helping a Jeweler serve her customer better. They are not just entering an order or packing a box; they are helping a Jeweler build a successful life and business. I want them to see the purpose and the meaning of everything they do, no matter how mundane it may seem. People find more energy and enjoyment in their work when they see that they are part of a much bigger picture.

What keeps a Jeweler going who has just had her tenth Home Show cancellation or postponement? Or what keeps a Jeweler going who has achieved all of her financial goals? It is the vision of serving and caring that she shares with the other Jewelers in her Premier Family and with the Associates in the Home Office. She is part of a bigger purpose.

When we need to hire personnel for the Home Office, part of the interviewing process, of course, is telling the applicant what the Purpose of our company is all about. If I talk to them personally, that is all I talk about. I don't talk about job title or job descriptions, resumes or opportunities for advancement. Instead, I talk about our shared commitment to serving others. If they don't get excited about that, then Premier is probably not the place for them. We want employees with a heartfelt commitment to this way of doing business.

Unlike most direct sales companies, we do not hire our Field Leadership from the outside. All of our Leadership starts off the same way—carrying a sample jewelry kit. All of our Leaders walk the road of experience and understand the reason we exist. They share our Philosophy that serving and caring bring rich blessings and total fulfillment, and they have experienced it for themselves. Developing our own Leadership from within is essential if we are to maintain a company-wide commitment to our vision of serving and caring.

When a Jeweler invites someone to join Premier, this same commitment is necessary. Our Jewelers sponsor people one at a time. When they invite someone into this business, we insist that they nurture them, encourage them and work with them. They must spend the personal time necessary to train them and infuse them with our Philosophy, Purpose and guiding Principles. We believe that it is our commitment to this shared vision that keeps us strong.

PRINCIPLE #4: CONTINUE TO IMPROVE

At Premier, we welcome complaints! Compliments are nice and we are happy to get them. We all like to hear when we are doing a good job and when we have made a difference to someone. However, we don't learn how to improve when everything is going smoothly. We learn how to improve from problems. I have found that we get some of our best ideas about how we can improve our service, our product, and our procedures from dissatisfied people who had the courage to say so. A problem is an opportunity to improve.

Premier is far from perfect. We have many areas where we could do better. That's not to say that we are doing a bad job or that we are a poorly run company, because we're not. It is just to emphasize that we are always on the lookout for ways to improve.

For example, we are constantly looking for ways to improve our customer service. We decided one way to do this would be to give our Jewelers better access to our customer service. So we gave toll-free phone numbers to all the major departments related to serving our people more effectively. Our hope is that this will result in more personalized service.

Additionally, our Jewelers brought to our attention ways in which the use of their personal computers would simplify their paperwork and ordering process. After much research, we instituted an online ordering program and have participated in the development of order software. I could give many more examples, but the point is that such changes are all guided by one principle: our commitment to finding ways to improve.

In summary, we have four guiding Business Principles at Premier Designs that affect our decision-making, our policies, our planning and our operations. We ask ourselves these questions: *Are we putting people first? Does this reflect careful financial planning and does it promote slow, controlled growth? Are we advancing the company's commitment to a shared vision of serving and caring? Is there some way we could do this better?* In order for these guiding Principles to guide us day by day at Premier, there are also some management activities that must be implemented. I call this our POSDA Plan.

1985 Founding Verse

"The Lord demands fairness in every business deal. He established this principle."

Proverbs 16:11, TLB

"The Lord grants a treasure of good sense to the godly....Wise planning will watch over you. Understanding will keep you safe."

Proverbs 2:7, 11, NLT

CHAPTER ELEVEN

Management Activities

eyond the principles that guide day-to-day business at Premier Designs, there are also management activities that are crucial to the effective implementation of these principles. I refer to this management strategy as *POSDA*.

PLAN

I believe in prayer, and we do pray at Premier Designs. Not only do we pray as Managers at the Home Office, but we also have committed Prayer Partners all around the world praying for every aspect of our company and its operations. However, as much as we pray, we plan more. I believe there is a time when God makes clear our responsibility, and we must think and then act.

Planning is an important function for us. It is our road map to the future. We plan for the short term and the long term, for the Home Office and Distribution Center and the field.

We have plans for five years from now, as well as plans for this week, this month and this year. Our business plans encompass all aspects of our operations, from anticipating building and physical plant needs to forecasting leadership and training needs. We plan financially with a yearly budget that is reviewed twice more throughout the year, and with daily and weekly appraisals of cash flow. We plan so we can control our growth, avoid debt, and make sure that we have and *will* have everything in place to be able to serve and support our Jewelers.

ORGANIZE

Obviously, a well-organized operation is more efficient and effective than one that is in a continuous state of chaos. Therefore, it is always worth the effort to get things organized and running smoothly. At Premier, we organize around the principle of serving our Jewelers. Home Office departments are structured according to the areas of service that we provide. In fact, every department's name has "services" in it, and every Manager oversees some area of "service," such as Financial Services, Jeweler and Customer Services, or Marketing Services.

Our procedures and staffing are determined by what will serve our people best. For example, we have organized and staffed our Home Show processing and order-filling operations to achieve the shortest time cycle possible for the Jeweler and her customers. Each aspect of the process is well defined, the Associates are well trained, and the goals are made clear to everyone involved. We organize and staff our Financial Services, not to make it easier on us, but to provide the Jewelers with their commissions and reports in as timely a fashion as possible. And it is never organization for organization's sake, but rather organization to provide more efficient service. As the Jewelers' needs change, so does the organization.

SUPERVISE

A well-managed company is a well-supervised company. It is important that we watch over and direct our Associates. Managers must oversee their departments and be aware of what is going on in each area. However, to supervise does not mean to boss, control or intimidate. Supervising well ultimately means building and sustaining relationships, letting people know that they are an important part of the team, and reassuring them that their job is secure.

We do not lead by fear or intimidation at Premier Designs; we lead by caring, by serving and by example. This doesn't mean that we don't care about job performance. We evaluate job performance on a regular basis and care enough to expect every Associate to do their very best. But caring also means that supervisors keep in close touch with their people; know how they are doing; and let them know what they do well, what can be improved and how valuable their contribution is. We expect the best from everyone and recognize that everyone, no matter what their job is, plays a role in our success.

DIRECT

To direct means to "determine the course of," and at Premier this management function is crucial. We must be faithful and diligent in making sure the company stays on course, in line with our Philosophy and Purpose. We must keep our focus on our Founding Principles of honoring God and serving people. Management and Leadership must communicate the vision of Premier consistently, and must walk it, not just talk it. We must guard against any erosion of our values and make sure that all decisions are measured against our Principles, Philosophy and Purpose.

When we have to make decisions, we determine our course by doing "what is right and what is best for Premier." We have repeated this phrase so often that it is now abbreviated as WIR-WBP, and everyone knows that we are referring to our basic principle for decision-making!

APPRAISE

Frequent appraisal of every aspect of Premier's operation is crucial. We need to know where we are and how we are doing if we are to make sure we get where we want to be. We look at our financial indicators at least weekly, and often on a daily basis. We close our month's books within a few days so we know exactly where we are financially. We regularly evaluate contests, promotions, paperwork and procedures to determine what works for the Jewelers and what doesn't. We are continuously evaluating our service, training, product quality and customer satisfaction.

Plan. Organize. Supervise. Direct. Appraise. This is the POSDA plan for managerial action, and it works.

You have heard how Joan and I started Premier

Andy at age two in Belfast, Ireland.

Joan's baby picture, born in Woodstock, Ontario, Canada.

Above: Andy's boyhood home on Upper Charleville Street, Belfast, Ireland.

Left: Andy's mother, Sarah, in Woodstock, Ontario, shortly before her death in 1947.

Above: Andy's mother's grave site in Woodstock, Ontario. The inscription on the headstone reads, "It is no vain thing to wait upon the Lord."

Left: Bill and Mary Blair and their children. The Blairs were the first people Andy and Joan met when they arrived in Dallas in 1950. The Blairs helped Andy find a job. They became life-long friends and the Horner's best "cheerleaders."

Above: Andy at age four with his mother, Sarah, in Belfast, Ireland.

Left: Andy with his brothers (L–R) Hugh, Andy, Sam, Tommy, Bill, and his sister, Chris (third from left) are shown here in 1982 at a Horner Family Reunion at Barrington College, R.I. Andy was one of thirteen brothers and sisters.

The *Duchess of Richmond*, the ship that brought Andy and his family to Canada in 1931.

Andy (center) and his fellow hockey team members in 1934.

Above: Andy at age 13 standing with fellow workers at the Maple Dairy in Woodstock, Ontario, where Andy worked as a bottle washer.

Top Inset: The apartment above the Maple Dairy where Andy and his family lived for 15 years in Woodstock, Ontario.

Andy and the Woodstock Y.M.C.A. basketball team in 1940.

Above: Andy with the 1934 Ford he and his mother used for their janitorial business. This car also won Andy a lot of friends in Woodstock, including Joan.

Left: The Woodstock Railway Station where Andy met the train and picked up the Toronto Star newspaper each day for delivery.

Above: Andy and Joan as teenagers in Woodstock.

Above: Joan's high school yearbook picture.

Left and Above:
Signalman Horner in his Canadian Sailor uniform in 1943, and the *HMCS Monnow*, the ship he served on during World War II.

Above: Andy and Joan's wedding on March 9, 1946.

Right: New St. Paul's Church in Woodstock, the church in which they were married.

Above: Andy and Joan standing in front of their first apartment in Woodstock, Ontario, in 1946.

Right: Andy, Joan and Andrea with their first new car, a 1952 Dodge. Andy jokes that this car cost him about $40,000 because he refinanced it so many times!

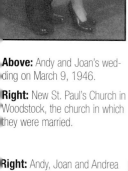
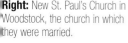

Right: The first home Andy and Joan owned in Dallas in 1954.

Above: Andy and Joan's home today, in Dallas.

Above: Andy and Joan's children in Racine, Wisconsin in 1961. (L–R) Mary, Tim, Tommy, Andrea, and Sarah.

Above: Horner family trip to Ireland in 1999 for Andy's 75th birthday.

Left: Andy and Joan with their family, Christmas 2008. **(L-R, seated)** Andrea Horner, Sarah Horner Wetzel, Mary Horner Collins. **(L-R, standing)** Tommy Horner, Joan and Andy, Tim Horner.

Right: Andy and Joan with their 16 grandchildren. **(L-R, seated)** Eric Billigmeier, Erin Billigmeier Figert, Joan & Andy, Jessica Horner, Justin Horner, JolieAnn Horner. **(L-R, standing)** Craig Callison, Grant Callison, Thomas Horner, McKenzie Horner, Kathryn Horner, Drew Horner, Lauren Collins, Miah Wetzel Confer, Johannah Wetzel, Caris Wetzel, Gabey Wetzel Blois.

Above: Andy with faculty of Criswell College on the occasion of Andy receiving his honorary Doctorate on May 11, 1986.

Below: Criswell College in Dallas. Andy has been involved in Criswell College since its founding in 1970.

Above: Andy and Joan with their Bible Study class, the "Humblelites."

Above: Andy's precious inheritance, his mother's Bible.

Below: Joan and her first Christian friend, Marie Hunter in Dallas.

Above Left: Andy, Joan, and Dr. Criswell in 1991 at the dedication of Horner Hall at Criswell College.

Above Right: Andy and Joan at the dedication of the Sarah Horner Rehearsal Hall in 1978 at First Baptist Church in Dallas in honor of Andy's mother.

Right: Hazel and Howard Goddard, life long friends, counselors, and prayer partners.

Left: Andy (far left) and the Johnson Wax leadership in Racine, Wisconsin, in 1961.

Below: Andy (bottom left) and the Xerox management in 1966.

Above: Joan, Mary Crowley (mentor, dear friend, and Founder of Home Interiors) and Andy.

Right: Andy, Mary Crowley, and Don Carter in August of 1972 on the occasion of Andy's promotion to Vice President of Administration for Home Interiors.

Left: Andy and the orphans of the Lar Evangélico orphanage in Portugal in 1987, a ministry dear to Andy and Joan's heart.

Below: Andy and Joan at the Home Office in front of the display of flags representing countries around the world in which Premier supports ministries.

Above: Andy (far right) and the Mission Directors of Word of Life in South America. The Word of Life ministry worldwide is a favorite of Andy and Joan's because of its far reaching ministry and its practice of training nationals to be missionaries in their own countries and around the world.

Right: Sophie Mueller with Joan in Venezuela. Sophie spent 50 years of her life in the jungles of Venezuela and Columbia translating the Bible and teaching the Word. Premier built a Bible Institute in Venezuela in 1993.

Left: Joan and the residents of the Doña Juana (named after Joan) efficiency apartments for married students at the Word of Life Institute in Argentina.

Right: One of Premier's projects is Lacken House, a 5-acre campus comprising the headquarters for Operation Mobilization in Rahara, Ireland. OM Ireland sponsors creative outreach programs for youth and Lacken House provides training and housing for evangelistic teams and volunteers.

Left: Andy and Joan with Drs. Paige and Dorothy Patterson at the ribbon-cutting ceremony for the Horner Homemaking House at Southwestern Baptist Theological Seminary in Fort Worth, Texas. The House provides classes for students working toward a B.A. in Humanities, with a concentration in homemaking.

Right: Another project close to Andy and Joan's heart is the new building for a church started by Bob and Sylvia Mulima with Transworld Evangelical Ministries in Uganda. Bob is speaking here at the dedication of the new building. The building will include a Bible school to train local pastors.

Left: Andy and Joan with their dear friends Andres and Mirta Fernandez Paz (left) and Joe and Melva Jordan (right), at the Word of Life Bible Institute, Schroon Lake, New York. Andres Fernandez Paz is the Co-Director of Word of Life in Argentina and Joe Jordan is the Director of Word of Life, Inc.

Premier's first Executive Directors (L) Randy and Elizabeth Draper and (R) Melissa and Greg Terrell, shown here with Andy and Joan.

Andy and Joan by the fountain that adorns the front of Premier's Home Office. The fountain was given to Andy on his 70th Birthday in August of 1994.

Above: Premier's Home Office Management Team. **(L–R, seated)** Linda Stefanides, Becky Williams, Andy and Joan, Debbie Walton, Gina Serrano. **(L–R, standing)** Lynn Hobson, Andy Bell, Virgil Jones, Kenneth Hays, Tim Helsley, Keith Gray, Don Cook, James Johnson, Tim Horner, Elbert Johnson, Bob Bolander, Kevin Moses, Dave Smith, Kevin Melton, Mike Glenn, Joe Call.

Insets above: Premier's first offices were at 3150 Premier Drive in 1986, followed by the second office at 2900 Gateway, and the third building at 3100 Premier Drive in 1989, all in Las Colinas (Irving, Texas).

Above: Premier's current offices at 1551 Corporate Drive in Las Colinas, on 12 acres purchased in 1993.

The 180,680-sq.-ft. Home Office facility includes offices plus the warehouse and distribution centers. A 67,995- sq.-ft. expansion completed in 2006 includes additional warehouse space for Premier, and larger storage areas for PCS Productions.

Above: Visitors receive a warm welcome from our Home Office Receptionists.

Above: The Hall of Flags displays flags from countries with mission projects supported by Premier Designs and the Horner-Premier Foundation.

Above: Top Jewelers are recognized for their achievements in a special display area at the Home Office.

Left: The Horner's extensive collection of Bibles is showcased in the Home Office entry to remind everyone that Premier Designs is built on Biblical principles.

Right: The Sarah Horner Chapel of Remembrance at the Home Office, named to honor Andy's mother, provides Associates and visitors a quiet place for prayer.

Left: The Historical Room serves to remind Jewelers and Associates of Premier Designs' early days and the reasons for the company's existence.

Right: Premier Designs' boardroom is where all decisions are measured against the company's Founding Principles, Philosophy and Purpose. Plans are made according to "what is right and what is best for Premier."

Above: In 2008 we modernized our Picking Line to a state-of-the-art automated picking bank.

Above: We pack each order in our signature gold boxes, but computers help keep track of every piece of jewelry, from inventory through shipping.

Above: Expanded warehouse space helps improve service as we grow.

Above: A cafeteria/break room and fitness center were part of the 2002 expansion.

Above: New 24,900-sq.-ft. gymnasium, opened in 2006, includes a walking track and a stage for company events.

Above: Although Premier Designs continues to buy from various jewelry manufacturers, our partnership with Premier Manufacturing gives the company an extra measure of product security and more control over quality assurance and inventory.

Above: Premier Communication Services (PCS) is committed to partnering with Premier Designs to honor God and enrich lives through their work on Rallies and special events, as well as training and motivational videos.

Above: The windmill at Haven of Hope was a gift to Joan from Andy for their 50th wedding anniversary.

Above: Rocking chairs on the porch of the Horner Lodge at Haven of Hope look out on a magnificent vista.

Above and right: The Haven of Hope *Empty Cross* sculpture is the center of the Prayer Garden located on Inspiration Point.

Above: The Premier Designs Singers entertain at the 2006 National Rally.

Left: Joan and Andy on stage at National Rally.

Right: Jewelers are recognized on stage at National Rally.

Below: Andy and Joan with Senior Leadership—Four Diamond Designers through Diamond Executive Directors at the 2010 National Rally.

Above left: Andy speaking at Rally during his "Lest We Forget" session, where every year he reminds people how and why Premier was founded.

Above right: "Have I told you lately that I love you?"

Left: Joan at Rally sharing from her heart with "Gems from Joan."

Below: Andy and Joan were awarded honorary Doctor of Humanities degrees in 2010, conferred by Dallas Baptist University and President Dr. Gary Cook.

and our founding vision. But Premier is not just us. It is a team of incredibly gifted people who have joined us in implementing the dream. I want you to meet some of the Team!

1987 VERSE OF THE YEAR

"Love is very patient and kind, never jealous or envious, never boastful or proud, never haughty or selfish or rude. Love does not demand its own way. It is not irritable or touchy. It does not hold grudges and will hardly even notice when others do it wrong. It is never glad about injustice, but rejoices whenever truth wins out. If you love someone you will be loyal to him no matter what the cost. You will always believe in him, always expect the best of him, and always stand your ground in defending him."

1 CORINTHIANS 13:4-7, TLB

1988 VERSE OF THE YEAR

"And now this word to all of you: You should be like one big happy family, full of sympathy toward each other, loving one another with tender hearts and humble minds. Don't repay evil for evil. Don't snap back at those who say unkind things about you. Instead, pray for God's help for them, for we are to be kind to others, and God will bless us for it."

1 PETER 3:8-9, TLB

CHAPTER TWELVE

The Field Leadership Team

Premier Designs does not belong to Joan and me. We did not build it alone. From the beginning this has been a team effort on the part of all those in our Premier Family. We could write another book telling the stories of people in our marketing organization, who have been with us from early on and who have played important roles in building Premier. Since that's impossible, let me introduce you to some of our key people—Premier veterans who are committed to leading Premier in the twenty-first century. As you read the stories of how they came to be involved with Premier, you will see a thread of God's design running through them.

※

MIKE AND GAYLE FOSTER

Serving in the Atlanta area, Mike and Gayle Foster have quickly risen to the level of Gold Executive Director. They received the Tom Hemingway Excellence in Leadership award in 2001, and Gayle became a part of our Royal Princess Court in 2008. Listen to Gayle tell their story.

If you had known me before I joined Premier, I would have been the last person you would have visualized selling high fashion jewelry. I had never been to a Home Show of any type in my entire life. I just had no interest. As far as the jewelry was concerned, I just never thought about it, and rarely dressed up enough to wear it.

I've always loved to compete. As I grew older and married, a new interest began to stir my competitive juices. I wanted a business that my husband Mike and I could own and develop. Hardly a day went by that we didn't dream about what we could do that would enable us to work together out of our home. There wasn't anything that could be sold, or any service that could be rendered, that we didn't consider. That is, anything except direct sales and home "parties." I would have felt more confidence performing brain surgery than I would have standing up in front of a group of ladies and giving fashion tips. I just couldn't see myself, in this lifetime or the next, doing a home jewelry show.

During this time, the unthinkable happened in my sister Janice's life. Through no choice of her own, she found herself left as a single mother with two little girls to support. As God is always faithful to do, He took the heartache and confusion and through it all miraculously brought the blessing of Premier Designs into her life.

As Romans 8:28 says, "God causes all things to work together for good to those who love Him, to those who are called according to His purpose."

What blew me out of the water was seeing my little sister able to totally support herself from the very first month of doing jewelry shows. I could not understand how my sister, who had never thought about any type of business, could be making more money doing Home Shows than I was making doing anything and everything but Home Shows.

Through Janice's urgings I finally "committed" with the most halfhearted commitment you have ever heard. My husband, Mike, was against it because of the questionable and manipulative techniques used by other multilevel marketing companies, and I was against it because I didn't want to ever do a Home Show. We came to a compromise: I would get into Premier just to get the wholesale-priced jewelry, but I promised Mike I wouldn't be gone more than one night a month!

Our lives were changed by two events. One, we went to our first Premier Rally. We could not believe what we saw. Mike saw a company that was completely different from any of the stereotypes he had formed about direct sales. At this "business Rally" we were spiritually uplifted and challenged. Our hearts were stirred by stories of changed lives, of families being brought together, and of testimonies from missionaries around the world who were being supported by Premier Designs.

The second event that changed our lives was when Andy and Joan Horner came to our hometown of Memphis for a visit. Andy shared why Home Shows are the heart of Premier. They aren't just a good way to sell jewelry. Home Shows are the best way to touch lives and spread hope. We both went away from that meeting realizing that God had indeed given us the home-based business we had wanted for so long, but with it He had also given us a vision for a ministry in others' lives, who would be touched through Premier.

Four years after that date our business had grown to the point where we could devote our full-time energies to Premier. We have been able to make far more money than any other business we ever investigated. We have made lifelong friendships. Together, we have been able to homeschool our two boys. God has used this company to give us "exceeding abundantly" more than we could have asked or thought.

⚜

KATHY AND TOM ALLEN

Kathy and Tom Allen became Jewelers in 1993 and achieved the level of Silver Executive Director in 2009, both demonstrating the gift of relationship-building that is so key in Premier. In 2002, they were the recipients of the Tom Hemingway Excellence in Leadership award, and Tom received the Mr. Premier award in 2004 and the Ambassador for Premier award in 2005.

In 1980, Tom and I had our first son, and by 1985 we had four more children—all girls. Tom was working hard, and I was home with the little Allens. I loved being a stay-at-home mom and felt that it was the very best thing for our children. I'll admit, however, that there were days I craved some adult interaction. I even worked several part-time jobs, but they never paid very much and were not very fulfilling.

In 1993, we heard about Premier Designs from Tom's sales manager, Rick Schwartz. His wife, Nancy, was a Jeweler in St. Louis. We lived in the Kansas City area, and I drove to St. Louis to meet Nancy and see a Jewelry Show. On the four-hour drive home, I wrote down the names of everyone to whom I'd ever said "Hi." I was definitely becoming a Jeweler. It was a very exciting and fun time! I was starting my own business; it was jewelry, it was fashion and it would work with our family life. I was going to give it my all. This was a decision that would change our lives.

I booked Shows around all the activities of our busy family. The Home Shows were so fun, and I was making really good income. About five weeks into the business, I had the privilege of attending a training conference in St. Louis. Andy and Joan Horner spoke, and it was a pivotal event for me. I learned that I was part of something more than just selling jewelry. They never talked about money; they talked about serving, expecting nothing in return. They talked about honoring God, and about the incredible opportunity I had to enrich lives. I left changed. I had a vision for more than just selling beautiful jewelry; I was going to make a difference in people's lives. I still remember coming home after that St. Louis Round-Up and telling Tom how different this company was.

From 1993 to 2000, Tom was my cheerleader and servant husband. He attended every event and Rally, supporting me and our Premier Family from the start. In October 1998, I became part of Premier's Senior Leadership team. I was so excited. Our business was growing, and people's lives were being changed. Amazing! Tom eventually left his job of twenty-two years to partner full-time with me in our Premier business. Being generous with the information and patient with the results is how we have built our business.

What I love about this business is that it is all about the people. People truly are our number one asset. Tom and I have grown together personally, professionally and, most of all, spiritually. I believed when I started, and still do, that being a Jeweler is the best! I work with passion because I believe in what I am doing. Our five children, who were ages seven to thirteen when we began this journey, are now in their late twenties. Our children have seen Mom and Dad work together and support each other, and this has given them a strong work ethic. We are both so thankful for this. I once heard a wise person say, "You cannot possess what you are unwilling to pursue." The future of our children is bright because of a decision we made years ago to join Premier. Our lives have been richly blessed.

෴

BEVERLY TERRELL

Beverly Terrell, now a Silver Executive Director, was sponsored as a Jeweler in 1988, by her son, Greg, and his wife, Melissa. Encouraging others seems to come naturally to Beverly and is one of the reasons she received the 2004 Tom Hemingway Excellence in Leadership award. She was named Premier Princess in 2005 and received the Marge Caldwell Encourager of the Year award in 2006.

It's always fun to remember that "ordinary day" that changed your life forever. Such a day occurred over twenty years ago when I phoned my husband, Jack, at his office to announce, "You'll never believe what I think God wants me to do. He wants me to join Melissa [my Daughter-in-Love] in Andy and Joan Horner's jewelry company!" Jack laughed and said, "God told me the same thing about three months ago, and I've been waiting for you to let God tell you!"

Three months before, Jack's company had been forced into declaring bankruptcy. He had promised every creditor that they would be paid, but there seemed to be no way to keep such a promise. When Jack saw Premier's unique Marketing Plan, he saw it as being our "Light at the End of the Tunnel" . . . and time has proven that he was exactly right!

I've heard it said that if you want to hear God laugh, just tell Him your plans for the next year. Well, I told Melissa and Greg that I would sign up, but I couldn't do Home Shows (I'd just sell jewelry samples from my hotel rooms, when I was on concert/seminar tours), and I wouldn't sponsor people into Premier (since I didn't have the time or the "know how" to sponsor). God laughed at my plans as He set in motion His own plans!

We began doing Home Shows, of course, and we earned enough money and sponsored enough people to have our company's bankruptcy dismissed within our first four years in Premier. It would've taken the average young couple a lifetime to do that. Incredible! What a mighty God we serve.

During our first nine months in Premier, Jack was diagnosed with an autoimmune disease (multiple system atrophy) for which there is no known cure. The following seven years we continued to do Premier together and enjoyed it more than we could've ever imagined! As we enriched hundreds of lives through our Premier business, those same lives continued to encourage and support us in every way imaginable. Our Premier business made it financially possible to meet his every need, even providing for a full-time nurse to live with us during Jack's final two years.

Our business grew and grew, but Jack and I were never driven by the goal to be rich. Yet, just as Joan and Andy Horner have set the example, I'm now also able to fulfill my own desire to share God's money with missions, churches and people in financial need, praying that we'll be "enriching every life we touch." From the day Jack and I signed our contract with Premier in July 1988, we claimed Ephesians 3:20 as our verse: "Unto Him, who is able to do exceeding abundantly above all we ask or even dream of, . . . to Him be the glory." And God *has* done more than we could dream through Premier Designs.

These are three gifted families who are key players on the Premier Team, and who have succeeded out in the field, and there are so many more. But Premier is not only the field organization—people doing Home Shows and building their personal businesses. We also have a committed Home Office team of Associates and Managers who serve and support the Jewelers in the field.

1989 VERSE OF THE YEAR

"Work brings profit; talk brings poverty!"

PROVERBS 14:23, TLB

࿇

1990 VERSE OF THE YEAR

*"Any enterprise is built by wise planning,
becomes strong through common sense, and
profits wonderfully by keeping abreast of the facts."*

PROVERBS 24:3-4, TLB

CHAPTER THIRTEEN

The Home Base Team

s Premier Designs has grown in the field, so has our Home Office and Distribution Center. We started out with six of us working in the office, and now we have over 200 Associates and Managers. We are fortunate and grateful to have such a strong team of Associates, people who really care about others and are committed to serving. I believe that God has each one at Premier for a reason.

Our Management Team is made up of people with a variety of skills and gifts. One remarkable thing to me is that we have never gone out looking for our Managers, or used "headhunters" or other agencies to find the people we needed. Rather, as a need arose, it seems that God had someone ready and waiting. The stories of how some of these people came to Premier are amazing, and I wish I could tell them all. I've asked a few of them to share with you their Premier stories.

JAMES JOHNSON, SENIOR VICE PRESIDENT AND TREASURER

In 1986 I was a comptroller and corporate officer of a hardware retail chain in Houston. I had been in this position for a number of years, but decided that it would be best for me to begin looking for another opportunity. We had some friends in Dallas who knew about Andy and Premier, and they told me to send in a resume. I did that in January 1987 but heard nothing back. So in February, I called Andy to ask about a possible position. He said he was headed out the door on his way to Houston to move into their new lake house on Lake Houston. If I wanted an interview, I could come by and meet him the next morning, Saturday, and that I should bring my work clothes.

So I showed up on his porch in my blue jeans and helped them move. As we moved boxes and furniture, Andy and I visited. I was able to see both the burdens and the challenges he was facing as he began this new company. I immediately knew I wanted to be involved. I knew I had something to offer Premier, but more than that, I was drawn to Andy's vision of serving others and helping missions. I felt I shared his values and that we had the same heart.

Andy didn't offer me a job that day, but the more I thought about the opportunity, the more excited I got. I drove up to Dallas on Sunday and showed up at the office on Monday. I was in the lobby when Andy walked in, and he was shocked, asking, "What are you doing here?"

"I came to Dallas to get a job at Premier, and I'm not leaving until I get one. I'll do something—fill orders in the warehouse, stuff envelopes—anything. All I know is that I'm supposed to work here!"

Well, Andy hired me. At first, I did a little of everything. Whatever needed to be done, I did it. I picked and packed, counted inventory and answered phones. We were all a team doing whatever it took to build this company.

After eight or nine months, the company had grown to the point where my work was primarily in the accounting/financial end. Over the years, it has become even more specific, having to do with the set up and operation of the Horner-Premier Foundation, and other projects close to Andy's and Joan's hearts. I am where God wants me, doing God's work at Premier, and I never plan to leave.

※

KENNETH HAYS, DIRECTOR OF PROCUREMENT AND QUALITY SERVICES

After I finished college, I worked in the insurance industry. As a hobby, I bought and sold land and timber. After five years of doing that on the side, I was making more money in that business than in insurance, so I went into it full-time. I got into land, timber, oil and gas, and mineral rights, and did very well. We invested in some other businesses, and they also prospered. Things looked good. My wife, Dardy, and I had everything we wanted—a nice home, nice cars, nice country club lifestyle.

In the early 1980s, I invested in an importing and distribution opportunity that looked promising, but which went sour. I had tied up a great deal of my own money in the deal and lost it all. That, coupled with oil, gas, and real estate all bottoming out in the mid-1980s, brought things to a head. Within five years, we were totally wiped out. I didn't tell Dardy. I thought it was my problem to solve, and I wanted to protect her from it.

By the summer of 1988, however, when our home was in jeopardy, it was impossible to keep our dire situation from her. Dardy began substitute teaching and tutoring after school. I took jobs here and there, whatever it took to put bread on the table. Just before Christmas 1988, we had to move out of our beautiful home. We even had to borrow the truck to do that. Things looked grim. Lawsuits loomed against us, and friends snubbed us. We sold off most of our furniture and valuables, just to pay our bills and buy groceries.

Then that spring Dardy was invited to a Premier Home Show. The Hostess told her that she should come and consider getting into this business. Well, Dardy wasn't about to go to this show. She hated "fake" jewelry and home "parties." Plus, she had students to tutor during the time the show was scheduled. The Hostess persisted in her invitation, Dardy's students canceled, and I insisted she should check it out. So she went. Later, a friend paid Dardy's way to Houston for a meeting where she could hear more about Premier, and she came home convinced. "I'm going to do this!"

We had one major problem, however—it cost money to get in. We had sold almost all of our things just to live. We had only one thing left— a brass-and-glass dining room table and chairs that Dardy loved and had hoped we could save. We sold it at an auction for three thousand dollars, bought our kit, paid our rent and utilities for the month, stocked the pantry, and went to work. We literally used our very last asset to get into the business. We knew we had no choice but to succeed.

Dardy had her training show April 20, 1989, and never looked back. Dardy was number one in the nation in sales for June, July and October, and consistently in the top five for the entire year. I was impressed with the immediate cash flow, but still a little skeptical about this company that seemed too good to be true. I was finally convinced that Premier was different when they sent an overnight package to our house on Christmas Eve, so we could get it to our customer for Christmas.

In early 1990, we began to feel that God was leading us to move from Mobile to Dallas. We didn't know why we felt so strongly, but we talked about it, and I started pursuing a couple of job leads there. We set August 15 as our move date, but didn't tell a soul. We went to Dallas in late June to find housing and make arrangements to move. It wasn't a week later that Bruce Peterson called us in Mobile and told us that the office manager had left. He said Premier needed an experienced office administrator. An hour later, Andy called and asked if I would be willing to come to Dallas to the Home Office and help them part-time with administrative duties while still helping Dardy with her business. Of course we had already made plans to move August 15, but he didn't know that! I told him I could start on August 16.

There have been a number of transitions since that time. Dardy was the National Training Coordinator for two years, but has now returned to the field building her business, with great success. My job has evolved from a general management position to Director of Procurement and Quality Services. I take my job very seriously. I know what Premier means to folks. I know it can mean the difference between feeding your children and not feeding your children. It made the difference for us.

⚘

BECKY WILLIAMS, DIRECTOR OF CUSTOMER AND RECEPTION SERVICES

I was lying in a hospital bed, recovering from a miscarriage of twins. I had been out of surgery one hour when the phone rang. My husband took the call; it was from my employers. The three high-powered executives of the international company where I worked wanted to know how long I was going to be out. They said they needed me to come in immediately to write a proposal for a meeting the next morning. I sighed.

I had worked for these people for over a year, putting in long hours, running errands all hours of the day and evening, with a husband and a two-year-old at home. I was a hard worker, never complained and always had a positive attitude. It was an important job, and I was the only Christian in the office. I wanted to be a beacon of how a committed Christian could excel and bring strength and stability to work. But I was under tremendous stress.

We began to pray that God would either give me peace about working for them or show me where He wanted me to serve. I had to work. Just the year before, my husband and I both lost our jobs when our company shut down local operations and moved out of state. We also had recently purchased a home, had a baby at home, and my husband had started his own fledgling business.

We prayed without ceasing. I updated my

resume, and with conviction included that my desire was to serve the Lord in any company for which I worked. Two weeks later I received a call from a friend who had toured the Premier Home Office as a vendor. He said he heard they needed a very organized multitasker to work for three managers and back up the president's administrative assistant. I faxed my resume that morning with a cover letter, explaining how I heard about the position. Less than an hour later I received a call from a very excited Ed Creek in the Personnel department. He said they had been praying specifically in a Manager's meeting that morning for exactly the type of person they wanted. After the meeting, he found my resume sitting on his chair. God's timing was perfect. Amazingly, everything on my resume was just what they had prayed for. Ed went into Andy Horner's office and told him about it.

I interviewed that afternoon, and to my amazement, I was asked to come back the next morning to meet the Horners. We went into Andy's office to talk, and he asked, "Would it be okay to pray before we start talking?" Well, that was it—I felt perfect peace and knew that it was God's design for me to be at Premier. My first day of work was September 23, 1991—the first day of a National Rally. Andy and Joan wanted me to understand what Rally was all about and meet the Jewelers. So my husband and I were both invited. What a first day at work that was, seated next to the wives of my new bosses! This was truly a family company.

I worked before for ten years in corporate America learning how the world works and does business. Now that I'm at Premier, I see how God wants a company to work and do business. God has taught me so much through many jobs in various Premier departments over the years. It was a great honor being promoted to Management under Andy and Joan. No two people could have been greater mentors or more incredible role models than they have been for me. I have always desired to use my God-given skills and make a difference in people's lives. It is a thrill coming to work every day, knowing we can serve everyone who calls, and that what we do and say can make a difference in someone's life. What a joy to serve God in a company that honors Him and people above all else.

ꝯ

THE MASTER DESIGNER

These are just a few stories of how God, the Master Designer, put together our Premier Home Office team. I can think of a couple more. When we needed someone to head up our Personnel Services, the perfect man for the job lived right across the street from us: Ed Creek. As a CPA, Ed had impressive accounting and managerial experience with Big Eight accounting firms, but the mid-1980s had been a time of personal and financial crisis. In Ed's words, "I went from the top to the bottom in six short years. I lost everything." I invited Ed and Janice to our very first Opportunity Presentation in 1985, but they had been burned by other direct sales companies so were reluctant to join us. When they decided to sign up as Jewelers in August 1989, I was delighted. Then, toward the end of that year, I realized that I needed help with personnel issues and thought of Ed. He had extensive experience and skills and a true gift of insight and caring for people. Not only has he organized and developed our Personnel Services, he also began our Prayer Services department for Jewelers and Associates. God had just the right man at the right time.

When I was first thinking of writing up the story of Premier in a book, my daughter Andrea was ready for a career change and available to come to Dallas. Not only did she spend much time researching and writing, but she also assumed the position of Special Projects Services Manager, producing and organizing our Rallies and special events until 2004. Joan and I had been planning and coordinating all those events, but it had become too big a job for us. God knew our need and met it.

Our Home Office Management team has expanded and seen many changes over the years. As Premier has grown, so has the need for skilled Managers to lead important areas of the Home Office, so that we can serve our Jewelers. These Managers have servant hearts and I am honored to be their C.S.O. (Chief Servant Officer). If we could tell the story of every

Manager and Associate, you would see how blessed we are with people who have the talents, the skills and the experience that we need—and you would see how each of them arrived just when we needed them.

Joan and I could never have done this alone. I believe we have the best Home Office Management Team of any direct sales company in America, because every member of our team has been brought to Premier by the Master Designer—at exactly the right time and with something specific to contribute. There are no accidents. This is not the luck of the Irish. This is by design.

PART THREE

The Growth of Premier

1991 VERSE OF THE YEAR

"Seven things for us to apply:
1. Love each other.
2. Honor each other.
3. Never be lazy in our work.
4. Serve the Lord enthusiastically.
5. Be glad for all God is planning.
6. Be patient in trouble.
7. Be prayerful always."

FROM ROMANS 12:10-11, TLB

1992 VERSES OF THE YEAR

"The person who knows right from wrong
and has good judgment and common sense is
happier than the person who is immensely rich!
For such wisdom is far more valuable than
precious jewels. Nothing else compares with it."

PROVERBS 3:13-15, TLB

"How much better is wisdom than gold,
and understanding than silver!"

PROVERBS 16:16, TLB

CHAPTER FOURTEEN

Home Office Growth

o serve our expanding number of Premier Designs Jewelers, we have expanded the Home Office facility in Dallas. After two years of planning and construction, the new building addition was completed in November 2002. We now have well over 180,000 square feet of space. If you come to Dallas, be sure to visit the new Distribution and Warehouse Center and the expanded employee facilities. Here is a preview of what you will see.

THE DISTRIBUTION CENTER

We have almost 30,000 square feet for our Distribution and Warehouse Center. This additional space has helped the operations process immensely. For example, the packing department was able to go from eighteen packing stations to forty stations, with two shifts. This translates into the ability to have up to eighty packers working each day, serving our Jewelers by making sure an order has been carefully filled and boxed for shipping.

EXPANDED EMPLOYEE FACILITIES

Growth means more than increasing physical space. It also means hiring more Home Office Associates to fill the many departments we have that serve Jewelers in the field. Because we want to enhance the emotional, spiritual and physical needs of our Associates, we expanded the Home Office to include a beautiful new 10,000-square-foot Health and Fitness Center. The Fitness Center offers cardio and weight training equipment, space for aerobics classes, a running track, a court for racquetball and basketball, plus free counseling on diet and fitness. The Manager of the Center develops individual workout plans for those who want them. Our Associates are enthusiastic about the Fitness Center and take advantage of this facility and its programs each day. What a blessing to have this for our Home Office Family.

But it's not exercise alone that helps our Associates stay mentally and physically fit. They need to eat well, too, and that explains the beautiful new cafeteria we added, with an industrial kitchen and a spacious eating area and break room. Tasty, healthful, reasonably priced breakfast and lunch meals are offered each weekday.

PREMIER DESIGNS SERVES IN SPANISH

Along with our facilities, a number of Home Office-based programs have also grown. One program we have implemented seeks to serve the Spanish-speaking community. You don't have to live in Texas or Southern California to see the growth of the Hispanic culture and the special contributions they are making in our country. In 2002, it was time for Premier Designs to learn to speak Spanish, and to offer our beautiful jewelry and our powerful opportunity to this important part of our population. We contracted with a Spanish consultant to explore the possibilities and give us an honest evaluation of the level of interest.

The enthusiasm of the Spanish-speaking population for the Premier Designs opportunity was off the charts, especially in the Southwest. We responded by translating many of our materials into Spanish. We also ensured that we had Spanish-speaking Associates in every department that has contact with the field. Now, when Spanish-speaking Jewelers call, we are ready to serve them in their language.

We stay in close contact with this new community of Jewelers, doing everything we can to help them grow their businesses and serve others. Our goal is not to create a separate Spanish-speaking division or company, but to bring these Jewelers into the Premier Designs Family so they can join us in enriching lives across America. We anticipate that this community will be an important part of our growth in the future.

HISTORY HIGHLIGHTED AND A CHAPEL BUILT

Another aspect of our expansion and growth in the Home Office involves honoring the past. History is so important, and we must remember and learn from the past. So before our large building addition was done in 2002, we created a Historical Room—a beautiful display area highlighting events and items of Premier's history. We did this so that Jewelers will always be reminded of Premier's early days and the Reasons for our Existence. We added a Hall of Flags to represent the countries of the national and international missions that the Horner-Premier Foundation supports. A display of my collection of old Bibles was also set up, to remind us of the importance of God's Word and that Premier is built on Biblical Principles.

Then we built the Sarah Horner Chapel of Remembrance, dedicated to the memory of my mother, who made that incredible decision to bring me to Canada. She laid the foundation of my moral and spiritual life. My mother spent her life serving Jesus and others. She lived out in the daily business of life what are now our core values—honoring God, serving others and enriching lives. Though she was an Irish scrub lady, uneducated and poor, Premier Designs would never have happened without her legacy.

Why a chapel? It is to impress others? No. Is it to make us look holy and religious? No. Is it to make us feel better than others? No. My nature almost always rebels against religious formalities. However, the thought of a chapel was something I had dreamed of and thought about for a long time. Several things sparked the desire to have a chapel in our company headquarters. One of the major reasons we have a chapel is due to our dear friend, Mary Crowley. I mentioned earlier about the special years Joan and I worked with her at Home Interiors and Gifts, and how much she influenced our lives. Whenever I talk about the Founding Principles of Premier Designs, I can hear Mary's voice. She is the one who taught me many of these basic values, and she had a beautiful personal chapel built beside her home, which we had visited. I remember she had one of her favorite verses inscribed on the front:

Thus saith the LORD, "Let not the wise man glory in his wisdom, neither let the mighty man glory in his might, let not the rich man glory in his riches: But let him that glorieth glory in this, that he understandeth and knoweth me, that I am the LORD which exercises lovingkindness, judgment, and righteousness in the earth: for in these things I delight, saith the LORD." (Jeremiah 9:23-24, KJV)

Through the years, Joan and I were exposed to other corporate chapels, which kept the idea alive for us. I was influenced by the Old Testament story of the Israelites. After wandering in the wilderness for forty years, they were instructed to build a tabernacle—a temporary place of worship—where God would dwell with His people and where His glory would be seen. And finally, we wanted to have a place that would serve as a continual reminder to our Premier Designs Family of our passion for missionary work around the world. I believe my strong desire to be involved in Christian missions came about because of my mother. She loved to support missions and often brought missionaries home to our little apartment. She also taught me the importance of giving financially to make missions possible.

Because of all these things, the Sarah Horner Chapel of Remembrance is a dream come true for me and Joan. We hope it will encourage any and all who visit it. We pray that through all the growth into the future, the Bible display, missionary flags, and the chapel will declare our love for and gratitude to God for all His blessings.

1993 Verse of the Year

"Be careful how you act."

Ephesians 5:15, TLB

1994 Verse of the Year

"For our people must learn to help all who need their assistance, that their lives will be fruitful."

Titus 3:14, TLB

CHAPTER FIFTEEN

A Haven of Hope

What is hope? It's the confident expectation that life will not end in tears, but in laughter. It is one of the priceless fundamental gifts that Jesus's resurrection gives to us, along with faith and love. We talk a lot about hope at Premier Designs. Back in the early growth years of our company, Joan and I dreamed about having a place where we could take Premier Designs people to give them a restful break and a dose of hope.

This was just an idea in our heads; there was no way that it could become a reality. As we struggled to rebuild our company in the early 1990s, we had no resources to purchase a training and retreat center for our people. Joan and I simply had to put our dream aside. Yet, God has promised that if we delight ourselves in Him, He loves to give us the desires of our heart (Psalm 37:4). The story of how our training center, which we named "Haven of Hope," came into existence proves this promise is true. It is not by chance that this beautiful piece of property is now used to give hope to thousands.

The story begins with Ruth Carter Stapleton, the late sister of former President Jimmy Carter.

A BEAUTIFUL PROPERTY FOR SALE

On Hilltop Road in Argyle, just south of Denton, Texas, Ruth Carter Stapleton owned a piece of property. Her vision was to create a healing center to minister to people both physically and spiritually. She made plans to develop the property into a place that she called "Hola Vida." However, she died of cancer before her plans came to fruition. An evangelical ministry purchased the property from her husband in the early 1980s. They renamed the place "Sonridge" and used it as their headquarters.

I served on the board of this ministry, and attended many board meetings there. I always loved walking through the trees along the ridge during our break periods. It was the perfect place to allow the breezes of refreshment to refill your sails. At the time, there was one large house and one smaller house that had a recording studio upstairs. (When we started Premier in November of 1985, I used this recording studio to record our first welcome audiotape. When you visit Haven of Hope, you can check out the old studio for yourself. It's still there.)

One day in 1991, as Joan and I were having breakfast with friends, they asked, "Have you heard? Sonridge is for sale." Well, we hadn't heard, but this news rekindled the dream. Could this be the special place we had dreamed about, a little haven of hope for our Premier Designs Family?

I could see that Premier Designs was getting back on track after the split in 1990, but we were only beginning to regain our stride. Our company was young and we didn't have the extra cash to be investing in property. Nevertheless, I couldn't get Sonridge out of my mind. One day, James Johnson, our Comptroller, drove with me to Argyle.

At the entrance, we passed a "For Sale" sign as we drove into what used to be beautiful grounds. It was now overgrown with weeds, the bushes were untrimmed, and the buildings were beginning to deteriorate. The property had been vacant for some time. When we returned to the office, we called the realtor and were told that the property consisted of 39 acres, two houses and a barn. The asking price was $650,000. We thanked him for the information and hung up the phone.

Whew! $650,000! It was time to drop this idea fast! I tried to counter with, "Yes, but property is generally a good investment," but I knew that this was not an investment that we could make at the time. It was time to forget the whole idea. I could not and would not put Premier Designs into that much debt. On the other hand, what could it hurt to call the owner of the property directly? So I did.

When he answered the phone, I told him that we were a company built on Biblical principles with the purpose of enriching lives across America. I explained that we were looking for a place where we could take people and train them, but more importantly, to give them a dose of hope. The owner replied that he liked these ideas and that he would like the property to continue to be used for ministering to people both physically and spiritually. He said he would think about it and call us back.

I don't know why I called or what I was expecting to happen. Humanly speaking, there was no way we could afford to purchase the property. But I had a feeling that God had a plan and was leading us. Indeed, as the rest of the story shows, God was up to something.

THE IMPOSSIBLE PURCHASE

Days went by, and we heard nothing from the owner. Two full weeks went by without a word, and I began to doubt that anything would come of my phone conversation. Then the owner's attorney called. "My client wants Premier Designs to have the property. We are willing to sell it to you for what is owed, $400,000, and we will take care of the realtor's commission." He went on to explain that for tax reasons, the owner did not want any payments that year, and that he wanted us simply to pay as we could over the next five years. Amazing!

In January of 1992, the papers were signed, and the property was ours. We immediately named it "Haven of Hope." It was the place that Joan and I had dreamed about—a peaceful country setting with no television or other distractions, a quiet place where Premier people could rest, get valuable training, and where they could learn and internalize our Premier Designs values.

Haven means "a place of shelter, safety and harmony." It is a place of beauty separated from the busy activities of the world. It is a place of peace and quiet, where you can see God's beautiful creation and feel the presence of His peace.

Hope is a basic need for the present and the future. It determines whether we live a life of fear or peace. Hope is something that abides with love and faith. It relates to what we believe and in Whom we trust. At Premier, Hope means "Helping Other People Excel." With these things in mind, we drafted a purpose statement for this new place:

> Our mission and purpose for Haven of Hope is that all who pass this way will be renewed spiritually and physically. We pray they will be touched by God's beauty, and that they will leave renewed—with hope in their hearts knowing that God loves them, and with a desire to reach out to serve others.

The purchase and naming of the place were only the beginning. Remember, the land had been vacant and much of it had gone back to nature. There was lots of work to be done, and Joan and I didn't want to move to the country and do yard work! Now that we had all this property, how were we going to get it back in shape?

JUST THE RIGHT CARETAKER

Remember the painful split in 1990 I told you about, and the lesson we learned that silence can be golden? Well, God has a great sense of humor—He used that difficult time to solve our caretaker problem for Haven.

When my former president started his new jewelry

company in 1990, he hired a warehouse manager named Don Stocklin. Now, Don attended a church pastored by my friend Bob George, who told Don about me. Don knew that his boss had once been the president of Premier Designs, and innocently, he asked his boss if he knew Andy Horner. "I've heard so much about him from my pastor. I'd like to meet him," Don said.

Don was fired on the spot just for mentioning my name! At that point, he decided that he really wanted to meet me! He made an appointment and came by our offices for a visit. The appointment just happened to be the day after we had signed the papers to buy Haven of Hope. He told me that he had graduated from Dallas Bible College and that he wanted to be in ministry. He also told me that he had extensive landscape and gardening experience. He loved the country. He loved working outdoors. And, he needed a job.

Do you think this was by chance? No way! I told Don about the challenge facing us to get this property into shape. I asked if he and his wife would like to become the caretakers of our new property and help us develop it for the Lord. They agreed.

There was an old house on the property up on "Inspiration Point," the second highest point in the county, with fantastic views for miles around. We fixed it up, and in March of 1992, Don and his wife, Lin, moved in. They quickly began to develop it into a place of beauty, filled with trees, gardens, flowers and grasses. They oversaw the construction process when we expanded from the original two buildings and a barn to seven buildings, and still counting. For Don and Lin, it was a work of love and service to our Lord.

Remember now, there was no way we could purchase the property when we first learned about it. Then, when the property was ours, we didn't know anyone who had the talent and dedication to do the hard work needed to make it into a place of beauty that people would enjoy. But there was Someone with a plan!

DIRECTORS FOR HAVEN OF HOPE

As the years passed, there were more buildings to build and more landscaped grounds to maintain. At the same time that the caretaking needs were increasing, there were larger groups using the facilities. This demanded a lot more scheduling and hosting to meet the needs of all the people who were coming. Don and Lin took on all this new work on top of the caretaking work that was constantly required.

After about eight years, they came to me. "Andy, we want to have a home of our own, off property. We need to be able to get away from the grounds so we can actually have a day or two off now and then!"

They were right. Joan and I realized that they needed more than an occasional day off; they needed help. We began praying for just the right couple to come along and help with the increasing load. We put a prayer request in our monthly letter to our Premier Designs Prayer Partners. That's all we did. In March of 2000, I received a call from Mac Bineham, one of our Prayer Partners, asking about the need.

Mac's wife, B.K., joined Premier in 1987. Due to

illness, she had to leave Premier in 1992, but she and Mac remained involved as Prayer Partners. Joan and I stayed in close touch with them. They were a great couple with servant's hearts and a missionary vision. Mac was considering retirement, and they were looking for an opportunity to be involved with missions. They wondered if this position at Haven might be it.

They came down, we talked, and after much prayer, Mac and B.K. became the Directors of Haven of Hope in November 2000. They were excited about serving Jewelers in Premier, and also about the opportunity to provide a place of renewal and rest for missionaries who would come there after their times of service overseas. They had the opportunity to enrich many lives during the training retreats, and to host many missionaries from many countries.

Do you think it was luck that caused the Binehams to be looking for a new place of service right when Don and Lin needed help? Do you think it was only by chance that they read the Prayer Partner letter just as they were planning to retire? By chance? No way!

CONTINUED GROWTH AT HAVEN

Haven of Hope now has seven buildings, with enough rooms to house, train and feed up to 100 people. All in all, the renovations have increased our space from about 6,100 square feet when we bought the property to over 37,000 square feet today.

In 2001, we added 43 acres, and in 2006 were able to purchase another 17 acres of land with a house, directly across the street from the original property.

We have added a full-size kitchen and hired Paul Nuss, a gifted chef. Paul and his staff provide home-cooked meals from a personalized menu, as well as maintain the property and buildings. And, by the way, we paid off the original debt in just three years, and every acre and all the improvements since have been paid for as we've gone along. God is so good.

Many other artistic additions have been made over the years. There is a large porch overlooking the view from Inspiration Point, for guests to sit and watch the beautiful sunsets. In 2004 an iron sculpture by Max Greiner, Jr. called *The Empty Cross* (a gift to me and Joan from the Home Office Associates) was placed in the lovely Prayer Garden atop Inspiration Point. There are benches scattered throughout the Garden, which were donated by our suppliers and engraved with our Verses of the Year. All in all, the Prayer Garden is a beautiful place for prayer and meditation, underscoring the purpose of Haven of Hope—to provide a place to enjoy God's beauty and to be filled with hope.

Since its beginning, thousands of people have passed through Haven of Hope. It's an operation that takes time and money, but what an investment. Many, many lives have been enriched and renewed with real hope. It is in use almost every weekend and during most weeks, too. There will be many more groups using the facility in the years ahead, and we are so pleased that our people have this facility to use. Our prayer is that when they leave, they will have hope and assurance, and will have caught the vision of serving and enriching lives.

Oh, I almost forgot to tell you about one more "lucky" thing. In 2001, geological surveys were conducted in the Haven of Hope area, exploring the feasibility of drilling for natural gas. You guessed it: they found gas, and productive wells are now operating! We signed an agreement and receive fees in exchange for drilling rights on the back side of our property. From what we understand, these royalties will help cover some of the operational expenses we incur at Haven of Hope. Even the Irish aren't this lucky! None of this was done by me; it was by God's design.

1995 VERSE OF THE YEAR

"Commit to the LORD whatever you do, and your plans will succeed."

PROVERBS 16:3, NIV

1996 VERSE OF THE YEAR

"And all the people were very happy because of what God had accomplished so quickly."

2 CHRONICLES 29:36, TLB

CHAPTER SIXTEEN

The Premier Manufacturing Story

uman beings find it easy to focus on the outward appearance—finding status or value in their clothes, jewels, accessories, car and bank account. The Bible reminds us that we are not to worry about the outer shell too much. "Your adornment must not be merely external—braiding the hair and wearing gold jewelry…; but let it be the hidden person of the heart, with the imperishable quality of a gentle and quiet spirit" (1 Peter 3:3-4). Notice it doesn't say, "Don't ever wear jewelry or fix your hair." It just reminds us that our inner character is what we need to focus on the most. Thankfully there's nothing wrong with wearing jewelry, which is a good thing. Because after all, Premier Designs is a jewelry company! Without jewelry there is no Premier Designs. Therefore, we have always highly valued the manufacturers and suppliers who provide our jewelry. In the early days of our company, we worked at times with over forty different manufacturers and suppliers. Most of them were based in Providence, Rhode Island. Then we began to see the effects of foreign competition. Because of low labor costs abroad, many of the American companies we worked with went out of business. Others were forced to move their manufacturing operations to other countries in order to compete.

We deal with fewer manufacturers now. We have worked with many of these companies since the beginning of Premier Designs and have built trusting and profitable relationships with each one. They know us and our market, and they play a major role in our beautiful, stylish line of high fashion jewelry. We appreciate them and their caring spirits as they continue to produce jewelry for us.

However, with so many manufacturers closing or moving out of the country, we had to take a strong look at our vulnerability. What would happen if any more of the companies we dealt with should become overseas operations, or if any more of them went out of business? One thing I felt strongly about was the need to stick to what we knew best. Premier Designs is a direct service company, not a jewelry manufacturing company. Joan and I had seen firsthand the skills and machinery needed to produce exquisite, quality jewelry. We knew that we did not have these skills or the machines. We did not want to get into the jewelry manufacturing business ourselves. Believe me, it's much more difficult than it looks, and requires skilled people and a lot of hands-on detail work.

THE START OF SOMETHING BIG

At that time, our son Tim owned a manufacturing company. He had built Weaver Manufacturing into a large, home accessory business, and part of their manufacturing process involved brass plating of the decorative metal items they built.

In the early 1990s, I was casually talking to Tim about some plating problems we were having with some of our jewelry. I also mentioned that we were having some quality and inventory issues as a result of the increased volume of our sales and the decreasing number of jewelry manufacturers. I wanted his input.

I knew jewelry is a tough product to make. The whole process is a very sensitive operation with a lot of costly handwork involved. But I was convinced that we should have our own manufacturing company, and he agreed. Tim is a strong, persuasive businessman, and he was convinced we could do it. Listen to the story in his own words.

※

TIM HORNER

In early fall of 1992, I accompanied Mom when she visited jewelry manufacturers in Rhode Island and Mexico. Subsequently, I talked with a number of people about starting up a company in Texas. All the experts told us it would be impossible to manufacture jewelry in Texas, mainly because all the expertise and know-how were in the Northeast, as well as most of the resources and equipment. I met many people in the industry and learned a lot. In spite of their opinion about our location, I decided to proceed.

In May of 1994, I hired our first employee, Wendy Waterman, who was very experienced in jewelry manufacturing. She went to work assembling our factory. We acquired a building, a computerized plating system and some experienced workers. In September of 1994, we received our first order from Premier Designs, for fifteen items for the January 1995 collection. By this time, Dad was also convinced we could make this work, and he saw the advantages of having more control over Premier Designs' manufacturing destiny as the company continued to grow. The legal partnership between my company and Premier Designs was forged in November of 1994, and Premier Manufacturing was born.

It's been a great partnership. We started small and learned as we went. We added a plating building in July of 1999 and another larger addition in the fall of 2000. We bought another 100,000-square-foot building on three acres, adjacent to the existing buildings. As of 2010, Premier Manufacturing has over 100 employees, state-of-the-art facilities, and produces and ships over seven million pieces of jewelry a year!

PREMIER MANUFACTURING GROWS

Tim has an outstanding management team in place and a creative and energetic product development team, who work every day on creating new products for Premier. In addition to the manufacturing area, they developed Premier Designs Incentives, a web-based business for online purchases of inexpensive items that Jewelers use in their business. It's been a big hit and is growing daily.

Almost every Friday, Jewelers visiting from all over the country take tours of the manufacturing plant. It is good for them to see what's involved in making jewelry. It opens their eyes and helps them understand how challenging the process is and how fortunate we are to have such a world-class facility.

Having Premier Manufacturing gives us product security should jewelry manufacturing continue to decline in America. It also gives us more control over quality assurance and inventory. But it would be unwise for us ever to depend on only one operation to supply our jewelry. We will continue to partner with our other current suppliers as well.

Our Premier Manufacturing partners are completely dedicated to the Philosophy and Purpose of Premier Designs. They believe in and understand the reasons this company was founded and are always seeking ways to serve our Jewelers. They will make sure we keep "looking good" with fine jewelry for years to come.

1997 VERSE OF THE YEAR

"The LORD says, "I will guide you along the best pathway for your life. I will advise you and watch over you."

PSALM 32:8, NLT

⚜

1998 VERSE OF THE YEAR

"For I know the plans I have for you," declares the LORD, *"plans to prosper you and not to harm you, plans to give you hope and a future."*

JEREMIAH 29:11, NIV

CHAPTER SEVENTEEN

The PCS Productions Story

As the company grew, so did the demand for communication and creativity. We needed to produce training media, such as audiotapes, videos and DVDs, as well as twice-a-year Rally productions, which involved staging, lighting, sound, site management and decorating. These Regional Conferences and National Rallies were becoming very large productions. Our growing communication needs demanded a lot of time and many gifted people in order for us to continue getting out our Premier Designs message effectively.

When we started Premier, Joan and I did most of the Rally production and media work ourselves. We enjoyed it. She worked on the decorations; I wrote the openings, prepared audiovisuals and designed the staging. Together, we lined up the programming, choosing skilled trainers to teach our people and guest speakers to lift their spirits. But when our Rallies began to have more than 1,000 people in attendance, and we began to have several of them a year, you can imagine how the preparation time increased. Many couples joined us, and they were a great help. But even so, by the time the Rallies arrived, Joan and I were so tired that it began to affect our presentations. It was time to get professional help.

First, we hired producers and directors. We let them know what we wanted and then let them take over. This was a great improvement, but it also created new difficulties. The production teams kept changing—sometimes their staff would even change mid-Rally. At times, the quality of the sound, the video work, or the stage management simply was not up to our standards. At the same time, attendance continued to grow.

With the ups and downs in production, the whole thing was becoming a source of increased mental strain for me. I realized I was not looking forward to the Rallies anymore. In fact, I was beginning to dread them. Joan and I continued to pour way too much time and energy into tending to the details of Rally production, when we needed to be concentrating on connecting with our people and communicating Premier Designs' message.

Our daughter Andrea took on much of the Rally responsibilities in 1992. We hired another manager a year later to help develop Rally programs. They were able to solve most of our problems in planning and producing the Rallies, but we still hadn't solved the problem of our need for a consistently reliable video team who could handle all the technical sound and lighting needs.

THE BIRTH OF PREMIER COMMUNICATION SERVICES

In the fall of 1993, our son Tommy left his job in the

manufacturing sector to start a video operation called "SportsCom." The purpose of SportsCom was to deliver high-quality coaching instruction via satellite to coaches all over the country. Tommy's new company produced an event in June 1994 that was broadcast from Reunion Arena in Dallas to more than 200 sites across America. By creating the coaching program and then delivering it via satellite, SportsCom was able to make skilled teaching available to coaches and players, both locally and all over the country. I'll let Tommy tell you what happened next, and how this became connected with Premier.

⚜

Tommy Horner

During that June event, SportsCom had high-profile coaches demonstrate their techniques, strategies and philosophies directly from the field of play for one hour. Then the folks at the remote sites could call in and speak directly with the presenting coaches. We also had a panel discussion, conducted by the Fellowship of Christian Athletes, relating the effects of drugs and alcohol on sports. After the event, we produced a 14-hour video series, which we offered to small college, high school and junior high coaches.

Our goal was to produce three to four coaching clinics each year and then continue to market the tapes. This is where Premier Designs first came into the picture.

For the initial broadcast in Dallas, we sold sponsorships to the likes of Nike and EastBay catalogs. Premier Designs also purchased some commercial time. I invited Mom and Dad to the local event at Reunion Arena, really more as a courtesy than anything else. I didn't expect them to come, but they came the first day and stayed for the entire event, from 8:00 a.m. to 8:00 p.m.! As we walked out of the arena, Dad commented that he had no idea I was doing such extensive production work and that he wanted to talk to me about helping Premier Designs.

In 1993, Premier Designs had moved into a 55,000-square-foot building, and in 1994 they still had some space they weren't using. I decided to rent the space to temporarily house SportsCom. This put us in closer proximity to Premier, allowing Dad and me to have a number of discussions about the Rallies. He shared with me how much they were spending to produce the Rallies, the difficulties of using a different production company each time, as well as his frustration with vendors who didn't understand Premier's Philosophy and the purpose of their Rallies. I had attended a couple of Rallies and wasn't that impressed with the quality of the production work. The more Dad and I talked, the more I thought maybe I could help.

On a Monday in early August of 1994, Dad called and said that he had just fired his Rally production company. He went on to tell me he wanted me to do lights, sound and video for the upcoming January 1995 Rally being held at the Dallas Convention Center, as well as all video pre-production. SportsCom turned a page as we began to work on Premier Designs' Rallies.

In March of 1995, Premier Designs formed a partnership with us to create PCS Production Company, LP. The PCS stands for "Premier Communication Services." It's been a great experience for us. We appreciate the opportunity to support and serve alongside Premier. We understand the reason why it was founded, and we believe in the Philosophy and Purpose of enriching every life we touch.

꙼

STATE-OF-THE-ART RESULTS

As Premier has grown, PCS Productions has grown. There are thirteen full-time employees and over 375 freelance contractors. Requests for audiotapes, CDs, videos and DVDs have also grown tremendously. PCS Productions has met those needs. They produce all of our training and motivational videos. They play a vital role in Premier Designs, and what a difference it makes! They help us with the planning, design and production of our Rallies, which are one of the major opportunities we have to build relationships throughout our Premier Family. It is at Rally that we gather people together for training, to share ideas and to get pumped up and renewed. Thanks to PCS, our National Rallies are professional and attractive.

Premier's expansion enabled us to offer Premier Communication Services much needed office and storage space. They built state-of-the-art editing and audio/video-production suites and a 9,000-square-foot world-class studio. The studio can be divided into a number of smaller studios, if the production schedule calls for that, or it can accommodate a large set and audience of up to 400. It is also versatile enough to host various Premier Designs banquets and meetings. In 2006, new dressing rooms and a 100,000-square-foot warehouse were added. Much of that space is used to store props, sets and Rally stage elements. This expansion has enabled PCS to serve Premier Designs Jewelers and Associates to an even greater extent than before. We're grateful to have them sharing the building with us.

Was it by chance that my son Tommy just happened to be skilled in media production and just happened to have formed a company to do this professionally? That at exactly the time his new production company was growing and needed office space, we had just moved into our new building? I don't think so.

1999 Verse of the Year

*"There is a time for everything,
a season for every activity under heaven.
A time to be born and a time to die.
A time to plant and a time to harvest."*

Ecclesiastes 3:1-2, NLT

2000 Verse of the Year

*"But they that wait upon the LORD shall
renew their strength; they shall mount up with
wings as eagles; they shall run, and not be
weary; they shall walk, and not faint."*

Isaiah 40:31, KJV

CHAPTER EIGHTEEN

Growth in Success and in Outreach

The company has grown and blossomed in ways we could never have planned or anticipated. We have had ever-increasing financial success and growth. Our first twenty-five years of growth are traced by the following graphs, which depict the triennial increases we've seen in the number of active Jewelers and the number of Home Shows. Remember, the bottom line in Premier Designs is not measured by business numbers. Our Purpose is to honor God and serve others. However, we also believe that if we keep these priorities in order, then our finances and growth will reflect that in a positive way. The reports from our Accounting department prove this to be true.

TRUE MEASURE OF SUCCESS

Premier Designs' financial success means food on the table for our Jewelers in the field, clothes for their

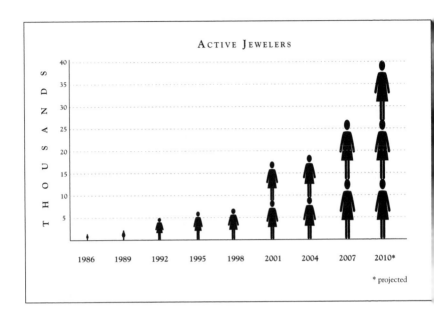

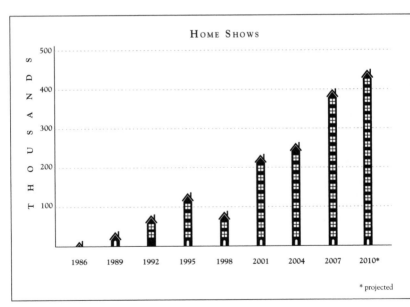

children, and college bills paid. What excites me the most about these charts, though, is to see the 450,000 Home Shows projected for 2010. That means that Jewelers will be invited into hundreds of thousands of homes across America! That's hundreds of thousands of opportunities for our Jewelers to serve with loving care, to meet people's needs, to share a dose of hope, and thereby to *enrich* hundreds of thousands of lives. That is how we measure success at Premier Designs. It's not the amount of jewelry we sell or the retail sales our Jewelers generate. It is the lives that they are able to enrich.

I believe there are few organizations in the world that have personally touched so many lives in so short a time, and we are just getting started. I want our success to continue to grow as we meet the needs of others.

One thing that is not reflected in these charts is the growing number of Senior Leaders we have—Jewelers who have reached the Four Diamond status or above. This means they have faithfully worked and built their businesses and are now part of our top Leadership. They are responsible to serve and encourage their down lines. These are the people who will carry our Philosophy, Purpose and Plan on into the second generation, ensuring that Premier Jewelers continue to serve in the homes of America with smiles on their faces and hope in their hearts.

SCHOLARSHIP PROGRAM

Our business growth is only part of the story of Premier. We also have a deep desire to support things we believe in, including education and our youth. Another aspect of Premier's outreach is our scholarship program.

Since 1990, Premier Designs has awarded hundreds of thousands of dollars in college scholarships to graduating high school seniors from across America. The one-time scholarship grants for tuition are available to children of all active Premier Designs Jewelers and Home Office Associates. To qualify, applicants must complete four essays, which are then judged by a chosen panel:

1. What I enjoyed most about my high school experience.

2. What I want to do and become in the future.

3. What America means to me.

4. What the most important thing in life is to me.

The essays are heartwarming and moving, and always give me hope for our country. We love to invest in the lives of young people; they are our future.

THE HORNER-PREMIER FOUNDATION

The Bible says, "God has given each of you some special abilities; be sure to use them to help each other, passing on to others God's many kinds of blessings" (1 Peter 4:10, TLB). Because we have been blessed with financial growth, we also have the privilege of spreading some of that extra success around. One of the main reasons we started this company was to support projects and ministries in America and around the world.

Hence, in 1992 the Horner-Premier Foundation was established. It is a self-perpetuating trust with a board of men and women who have the same beliefs and philosophy as Joan and I have. They understand the Purpose and Founding Principles of this company, and each of them is committed to these. The main purpose of the Foundation is to keep Premier Designs on course, doing what it was created to do.

The vision and purpose of the Foundation consist of the following:

- To be based upon Biblical Principles
- To enrich every life we have the privilege of touching
- To meet spiritual and material needs around the world
- To assure that the Philosophy and Purpose of Premier Designs never change
- To provide a vehicle to ensure that donated dollars are spent in a God-honoring way

After Premier Designs pays its vendors, commissions and Home Office Associates, and reserve funds are met, it contributes to the Horner-Premier Foundation. This contribution allows the Foundation to be a vehicle to maintain the core values of Premier Designs by supporting ministries and missionary families around the world. We are excited to support a varied array of projects in over forty countries of the world: youth camps, sports camps, orphanages, medical clinics, disability ministries, inner-city schools,

Countries where Premier Designs and the Horner-Premier Foundation
support Ministries and Missions Projects

Austria   Hungary
Czech Republic Poland
France   Portugal
Ireland   Romania
Israel   Russia
Italy   Spain
               Ukraine

USA

Cuba
Dominican Republic

Costa Rica
Guatemala
Honduras
Mexico
Panama

Argentina
Bolivia
Brazil
Chile
Columbia
Ecuador
Paraguay
Peru
Uruguay
Venezuela

Cambodia
China
India
Japan
Korea
Myanmar (Burma)

Indonesia
Philippines

Egypt
Ghana
Kenya
Nigeria
South Africa
Uganda

scholarships, colleges, churches, seminaries, Bible schools, urban renewal projects and much more. The map shows the countries in which we are involved.

The Horner-Premier Foundation will hold most of the company's voting stock after Joan and I have gone to heaven. Our Horner children clearly understand the reason Joan and I have set up the Horner-Premier Foundation, and they fully support what we have done. Our Home Office Management and Field Leadership also join in this commitment. The Horner-Premier Foundation will have tremendous influence on and control of the direction of Premier Designs in the coming years.

We have learned about the growth and expansion of our company and its partners, as well as the outreach we have with Haven of Hope and the Horner-Premier Foundation projects. Now, let's look ahead. In the next section I want to share from my heart about our design for the future.

PART FOUR

The Future of Premier

2001 VERSE OF THE YEAR

"Give thanks to the LORD and proclaim his greatness, let the whole world know what he has done."

PSALM 105:1, NLT

2002 VERSE OF THE YEAR

"Let your light shine before men, that they may see your good works and glorify your Father who is in heaven."

MATTHEW 5:16, NLT

CHAPTER NINETEEN

Maintaining Our Core Values

I was at one of the Premier Designs Rallies at the Fort Worth Convention Center a couple of years ago. After the excitement of seeing our new jewelry line for the next season introduced, one of our faithful Jewelers came up and asked, "Andy, what's going to happen to Premier in the future? What happens when you and Joan are gone?"

I'm asked this question a lot. After all, we are in our eighties. The truth is, only God knows the future. But let me share with you the steps we are taking to ensure that our core values will not be lost. There are strong reasons for me to believe that Premier's future will be great.

THE FIRST GENERATION

When Joan and I look at the founding generation of Premier Designs, we are blown away by what they have accomplished. Our Jewelers and Associates have enriched hundreds of thousands of lives. Moms have been able to stay home with their children because Premier Designs made it financially possible. Single moms have built their own businesses to provide for their households. Orphanages, inner-city churches, family ministries, ministries for the handicapped, and missions around the world have been supported—and I believe that all this is only the beginning. We are building together a strong foundation for the next generation—but we need to learn a lesson from history.

THE DANGER OF FORGETFULNESS

History has shown time and time again that the second and third generations of a company or an organization can stray from the original vision—and it can happen fast.

Harvard University was established to train preachers to proclaim the Christian gospel, but within one generation their founding mission was forgotten.

When our friend Tom Landry coached the Dallas Cowboys football team, his Christian beliefs and values influenced the image of the Cowboys as "America's team." When the team got a new owner, who fired Landry and hired a new coach, the entire image of the Cowboys changed. They went on to win five Super Bowls, but the core values—wholesomeness, integrity and serving as good examples for young athletes—largely disappeared.

J. C. Penney founded his company on Christian principles. It is still a great corporation, but the principles of the founder have been forgotten.

The headlong rush toward growth—bigger profits, bigger buildings and bigger opportunities to sell product—can be dangerous. This is especially true of a direct service company such as Premier. With rapid growth, you can lose control. And when you lose control, you risk losing touch with and *forgetting the company's heart and purpose.* Remember what I said earlier about the necessity of controlled growth? This is absolutely key.

We must never forget the basics that have made Premier Designs successful. Is the secret of our success Joan and Andy Horner? No. Is the secret of our success the uniqueness of our product, our Marketing Plan or our Hostess Plan? No. I believe our product and plans are the best in the industry, but they are not the secret to our success. Can our success be attributed to the skills and expertise of our Home Office Management Team? They are gifted and committed folks, but they are not the reason for our success. Then it must be our awesome Field Marketing Team! Of course, it must be our great Designer and Diamond Designer Leaders! I believe they are the best in America. They work harder and they serve with more heart than anyone else in our industry, but they are not the reason for Premier Designs' success. The secret of Premier Designs' success, both now and in the future, rests in our continued, unwavering commitment to our Founding Principles.

THINGS THAT MUST NEVER CHANGE

Premier Designs is built on a Biblical foundation—principles that are at the heart of all companies that last. Old-fashioned values such as honesty and integrity, the need to honor God and serve others, and the passion to enrich the lives of others—these are the things that must never change. I want my words to be recorded in your heart and played over and over: *Premier Designs is not about selling. It is about serving and sharing. It is not about product and profit. It is about people.* Mary Crowley taught me that when you build the people, they will build the business.

Now don't misunderstand me; Premier is a business, and it must be measured by the same criteria as any other corporation. We must manage our resources well and be financially strong. But we must always remember that there is something far deeper than these financial criteria that drive our success. Real success is not related to our possessions, position or status; rather, it comes from serving and enriching others, and that includes fulfilling and using the potential God has given us.

Please don't take this as a pious, religious thing to say, but the truth is that there is going to come a day when the gold in our pockets won't mean a thing. God uses it like gravel to pave His heavenly streets. Other people's appraisals of us will ultimately mean nothing. Matthew 6:19-20 (KJV) says, "Lay not up for yourselves treasures upon earth, . . . but lay up for yourselves treasures in heaven." There will come a day when visible assets such as beautiful homes, swelling bank accounts, luxury cars, beautiful clothing and, yes, even beautiful Premier Designs jewelry, won't be worth a thing. The Bible challenges us to keep our eyes on the invisible things—personal, moral and spiritual values— that will last forever. This is the reason we formed the Horner-Premier Foundation, in order to keep Premier

Designs on course, focused on supporting the spiritual values that will last.

What a privilege to be in a business where this real bottom line is emphasized! We are investing in people. We are investing in God's work around the world, and these treasures will be valuable forever. We need to be faithful and obedient stewards of the resources that God gives us. I love what Proverbs says, "Honor God with everything you own; give Him the first and the best. Your barns will burst; your wine vats will brim over" (Proverbs 3:9-10, MSG). We must always remember that Premier Designs and the material rewards that it brings are gifts from God.

AUTHENTIC, COMMITTED LEADERS

This leads us to the question: What's the best way to make sure we maintain the priority of these spiritual and moral values and our Founding Principles? It all begins and ends with our Leaders.

Our Leaders, both in the field and in our Home Office, must remain focused on the original vision of Premier Designs. They must believe in the truth and the power of our Founding Principles. Core values, such as "People are our most valuable asset," must guide their daily work and all the decisions they make for our company. Our Leaders, at every level, must know and internalize what I have written in this book about our Purpose and Philosophy, so that when new Jewelers and Associates join us, they "catch" this Premier heart from them. As our present Leadership passes the baton to the next generation of Premier

Leaders, they will ensure our future success and make sure that the Premier Designs vision is not lost.

It's Up to You!

If you are a Leader, your number one responsibility is to make sure that everyone understands and then lives out our Philosophy and our Purpose. As long as God gives us strength, Joan and I will continue to remind you to do what I am stressing in these pages. We will keep reminding you of the Founding Principles and Purpose of Premier Designs. We will keep sending you notes and giving you updates that stress how much God loves you and how much we love you. We will keep telling you in phone calls that God does have a marvelous plan for your life. We will spend the hours needed to build a Home Office Team and Field Marketing Team who are committed to our founding vision. Then it's up to you.

2003 VERSE OF THE YEAR

*"Choose a good reputation over great riches,
for being held in high esteem is better than
having silver or gold."*

PROVERBS 22:1, NLT

୬

2004 VERSE OF THE YEAR

*"Let us stop just saying we love each other; let us
really show it by our actions. It is by our actions
that we know we are living in the truth."*

1 JOHN 3:18, NLT

CHAPTER TWENTY

Remembering Our Biblical Foundation

When Joan and I started Premier Designs, we decided to build it on Biblical principles. Today, when leaders in our industry recognize and honor Premier and ask about the high quality of our people, our company's integrity and our service attitude, we point straight to the Bible. I always explain that all of this is the result of trying to follow God's principles for life and for business.

This doesn't mean that Premier Designs is a "Christian company." There's no such thing as a "Christian company." God has relationships with people, not businesses. There won't be any companies in heaven. Premier Designs is not a "Christian company" —it is a company built on Biblical principles.

What does that mean, to be built on Biblical principles? Well, for one thing, it means that the decisions made at Premier are based upon prayer, upon patience and upon counsel from others. Being founded on Biblical principles also relates to finances. We are a company with no debt, a company that builds with cash, a company that is committed to sound accounting principles. Those are Biblical principles. We operate with integrity and honesty, and conform to all laws. We say what is true and do what is right, to the best of our ability.

Because we are based on Biblical principles, people are more important to us than profits. It means that we care and seek to serve and enrich others, and that we give without expecting anything in return. When there are people with needs, we don't act with only the bottom line in mind; we do what is necessary to meet the need in that person's life. This is how we try to live and work according to principles found in the Bible.

Does this mean that Premier Designs is some kind of a religious group, denomination or missionary organization? Do we think we are holier than others are? Are we so heavenly-minded that we are of no earthly good? No way! We are simply a business—a company whose leadership takes seriously God's instructions in the Bible. This is where we got the idea to reach out and meet the needs of others. This is where we learned that every individual is precious and has eternal worth. This is where we learned that we must care. This is where we learned that leaders must first be servants. These are Biblical principles that guide us at Premier Designs.

Some people might say that being a company built on Biblical principles means that we are excluding those who aren't religious or who are of another faith, but that's not true. We will always share our hearts and will speak openly of our beliefs, but it doesn't matter if someone shares our beliefs or not—they are welcome in the Premier Designs Family. We will love them, respect them, invest in them and serve them because of who they are, not based on their faith, background, culture or race.

Now, please understand me. I'm not claiming that if you found your company on the Bible, it guarantees success. The Bible is not a magic formula. After all, the Bible itself stresses over and over that we reap what we sow. If we make bad business decisions, there will be bad consequences. If we fail to manage our resources well in the good years, there will be a price to pay in the lean years. We have to use our heads—and that's a Biblical principle, too!

WHY I BELIEVE THE BIBLE

Today, many people think it strange to talk about these spiritual values outside the walls of church. But throughout history, great men have attested to the truth and the power of the Bible and its impact on their lives. Today, many have chosen to reject the Bible, and many think of it as a book of myths and fairy tales. This, of course, is their prerogative. But I have chosen to believe that God inspired the authors of the Bible. God worked through their individual styles and skills, but they wrote exactly what God wanted us to know. Every word, every syllable and every thought is there for our good. Do I understand it all? No. If I did,

I would know that it must not be from God! As finite people, we shouldn't expect to understand everything that God has to say. I don't understand it all, but I believe it all.

When I was a small boy, I sang this chorus with my mother. Later, I taught it to my own kids. I still believe this today:

> The B-I-B-L-E
> Yes, that's the book for me.
> I stand alone on the Word of God.
> The B-I-B-L-E!

My mother believed every word in the Bible, and she claimed every promise. I saw how it affected her life. My older brother was an evangelist, and he often talked to me about Jesus and the Bible. As a boy, I was in Sunday school and church every time the doors were open. Teachers and famous preachers such as Dr. W. A. Criswell have taught me about the Bible, but all their teaching and preaching is not the reason I believe the Bible to be the inspired Word of God. It is because the God of the Bible has never abandoned me. As a young boy, I received Jesus, His Son, into my life, and He has never left me.

In the Navy during World War II, I strayed from my childhood faith. When I got out of the service and entered the world of business, I kept running from God. I shared with you earlier in these pages how in 1951 I rededicated my life to the Lord Jesus at the First Baptist Church in Dallas and started to walk with Him again.

Daily, I read the Bible and talked things over with

Him in prayer. It was this time of listening to God speak to me personally in the Bible that caused me to conclude for myself that the Bible is truly His Word. I realized I could trust it, and by faith I could apply it to my personal, family and business life.

I have experienced God's presence, love, protection and guidance. I have sensed His direction in my life and His peace and comfort in times when things were good, and also when things were bad. I have learned in the school of experience what the Apostle Paul declared as he neared the end of his life, "For I know whom I have believed and am persuaded that He is able to keep that which I have committed unto Him until that day [the day of Jesus's return]" (2 Timothy 1:12, NKJV).

And then Paul said, "For I am convinced that neither death nor life, neither angels nor demons, neither present nor future, nor any powers, neither height nor depth, nor anything else in all creation, will be able to separate us from the love of God that is in Christ Jesus our Lord" (Romans 8:38, NIV). Yes, that's what I believe, because those words have proved to be true in my life. Has my life been free from tough times and struggles? No, but the Bible gives me comfort and hope.

I can't persuade you to believe in the Bible. You will have to read it and look at the evidence for yourself. But I can say that if you have no lasting satisfaction and no real peace—if you feel like you're running on empty at times, then you should open your Bible and listen to what God has to say to you. The Bible has sustained me, and it will sustain the life of Premier

Designs as long as we remain committed to its truth.

One of the most amazing things Jesus ever said was, "I am among you as one who serves" (Luke 22:27, NIV). I had read that verse in the Bible over and over again, but it took God almost fifty years to teach me what it meant. That's what I want to talk about in the next chapter.

2005 VERSE OF THE YEAR

*"This is the LORD'S doing, and it is marvelous
to see. This is the day the LORD has made.
We will rejoice and be glad in it."*

PSALM 118:23-24, NLT

❧

2006 VERSE OF THE YEAR

*"Hope deferred makes the heart sick, but when
dreams come true, there is life and joy."*

PROVERBS 13:12, NLT

CHAPTER TWENTY-ONE

Serving Is Our Future

arlier in my business career I worked for a man who relied heavily upon my skills in administration, training and leadership, and then took credit for what I did. I didn't respect his morals or his bottom line. He made me pretty angry sometimes.

One day on my way to work, as I was praying again about my frustration with my boss, God quietly impressed something new on my heart: "Andy, I want you to stop fighting and competing with him. I want you to respect his position, and I want you to serve him with a willing heart."

Now, you know my story. If ever there was a man who wanted to climb from the bottom to the top of the ladder of recognition and position, I was the man. And now, God was telling me not only to stop on the rung where I was, but also to step off the ladder completely. He wanted me to go back and take the humble, low position—the role of a servant.

It's tough to be a servant. But I discovered that

you actually begin to have influence with others when you stop trying to get above them, and get underneath them instead. I went to work that day with one objective—to respect and serve my boss with a willing attitude and to try to meet his needs and follow his directives. In short, I set out to be his servant.

You wouldn't have believed the change in my spirit over the next few weeks. I'm not going to say that my new "servant" role radically changed my boss overnight. He remained the same bottom-line guy who used people, but my frustration with him began to diminish. For sure, it improved the atmosphere in our office, and I began to understand the paradox of Jesus's statement that if you want to be great, you have to learn to be a servant (see Mark 10:43). The real power lies in being a servant, not in being a lord.

BUILT TO SERVE

When Joan and I started Premier, we wanted to establish a company that would bless people, bless families, bless the Hostesses of our Home Shows, bless the Jewelers who entered their homes, and bless all our support people in the Home Office. The principle that could bring this blessing was the power of serving, so we made this a Founding Principle of our company.

We decided that we would stress *serving*—meeting the needs of others, not living for ourselves. We would teach that success lies not in how many people serve you, but how many people *you* can serve. Service—it defined our beginning and it will define our future. It's why we call ourselves a *direct service* company, with the

226

emphasis on caring for and serving others, not making money for ourselves. I have never talked about sales in all our years of business, but I have consistently talked about serving.

These days, everyone in business is talking about service. Our culture has moved from a goods-based economy to a service economy. The companies who succeed combine both excellence in their products and excellence in their customer service. At Premier, we stress both quality and excellent customer service. But we also strive to go a step further. I'm talking about a life commitment to being a servant. This is the heart of how Premier Designs defines success. It must remain our philosophy now and in the future.

A PHILOSOPHY OF SERVICE

Serving others is not an option at Premier; it is a must. A serving spirit must saturate every area of our company. Serving means that people, not product or sales, are our real bottom line. Serving is not a program. It is a way of life, and defines everything we do. What does that look like? Here's what serving means out in the field in our business:

- Taking Christ's example of servanthood seriously.

- Helping others, expecting nothing in return.

- Discovering that real success lies in bringing joy to others.

- Proving our service with kind attitudes and helpful actions.

- Helping people book and sponsor others in the business, but more importantly, building *continuing* relationships with our down lines, our Hostesses and our customers.

- Adding value to our product with the intangible values of personal service, integrity and caring.

Oh, incidentally, I almost forgot to tell you—you can't serve this way and *not* sell. I can tell you from experience that if you serve, you will have a financially rewarding business.

Our Associates strive to have a spirit of service, too. Implementing a servant's heart at the Home Office means that we:

- Put people first—not sales, production or the bottom line.

- Emphasize concrete ways to meet the needs of others.

- Have a person (not a machine) answer the phone, asking, "How may I serve you?"

- Make sure that systems and technology don't dictate what we do or how we treat people.

- Remain committed to our Home Show Plan, because Home Shows fulfill our

Purpose and allow us to personally meet needs and build relationships.

- ◆ Serve our Jewelers well, along with our suppliers and vendors. Service must remain our all-pervasive spirit!

THE PATH OF SERVICE

Premier Designs is different. When others emphasize selling, we emphasize serving. When others tell lies and falsify the books, we are committed to truth and integrity, no matter what the cost. When the business world encourages mothers to work out of the home, away from their children, we provide a way for them to conduct income-producing work from home so they can be with their children and still pay their bills. In a culture where you can get tons of information but no personal contact, we built our company around connecting with others, building them up and loving them. In this communication age, we stress loving actions not just words. We must live out loving service, not just talk about it. As it says in 1 Corinthians 13:13 (NLT), "There are three things that will endure—faith, hope, and love—and the greatest of these is love."

There is a fork in the road to the future. One fork is a path that will take us to power, prestige, money and riches, even as it takes away our heart. The other fork is the path we chose from the beginning for Premier Designs—the path of serving—and it is the path we must keep following to find real success and peace.

PART FIVE

The Proof of Premier

2007 Verse of the Year

*"I know, my God, that you examine
our hearts and rejoice when you
find integrity there."*

1 Chronicles 29:17a, nlt

2008 Verse of the Year

*"Show me the path where I
should walk, O Lord;
point out the right road for
me to follow."*

Psalm 25:4, nlt

CHAPTER TWENTY-TWO

The Purpose Realized

I'm sure that by now you have gotten our message: The Purpose of Premier is *To Enrich Every Life We Touch*. We want to enrich the lives of those who join our Premier Family, and we want them to catch the vision of enriching the lives of those with whom they come in contact—Hostesses, customers and each other. Most people join us for the money. They have financial needs, and this is their primary motivation at the outset. We want them to meet these needs. We designed a good payout on sales and a generous commission structure for that very reason. But there is more—and that "more" is serving others, caring and sharing.

Does it work? Are people's lives better because of Premier? Have our Jewelers caught the vision? Are they motivated beyond the money to serve others? The proof of the pudding is in the eating, and Joan and I have the privilege of hearing from so many about all that is happening in their lives. We could fill volumes with their Premier stories. Why don't you look over our shoulders for a few minutes and read a sampling of excerpts from the many letters we have received, so you can see for yourselves the proof of Premier.

Enriched by Personal Growth

Dear Andy and Joan,

When I joined Premier, I thought I would be selling jewelry to earn a little extra income. I had no idea how this company would help to change my life! Premier has given me the courage to be the outgoing, positive person that God intended me to be. My confidence has grown as I've stood in front of ladies at Home Shows. I now take better care of myself and take more pride in my personal appearance. The financial rewards have been wonderful, but nothing compares with the emotional gains. (Two Diamond Designer from Georgia)

Dearest Andy and Joan,

I thank God that He gave you a vision for Premier and that you obeyed His call. Premier has opened up a whole new world for me. I was a stay-at-home mom, a priority for my husband and me, with very few friends and extremely low self-esteem. After four years with Premier, I found that I could learn and do something that made me feel good about me. It built my confidence in myself, which I never had, and I began to like myself. (Jeweler from Mississippi)

Enriched by the Premier Family

Dear Andy and Joan,

You cannot imagine how you have touched my life. I look back at the past three-and-a-half years and am amazed by what has happened in my life. My first year in

Premier I didn't do much because of my Air Force job. I finally got going when hurricane Andrew came and wiped out all my material possessions. You, the folks in the Home Office, and my Premier Family were all there for me. It was amazing the love and support I received. You all kept encouraging me and telling me that God was with me. I had no money. I had no material possessions. But I had never felt so much love and peace. (Jeweler from South Carolina)

Dear Joan and Andy,

I joined "the Premier Family" in January 1991. It was something I never dreamed of doing, and it has made such a difference in my life. I am an only child and have lost my mom and dad. I have my husband and our four sons, but they are all grown. Premier has given me a new family that means so much to me. I love everyone in my Premier Family, and there is not a thing I wouldn't do for them. It has given me people to love and who love me, and something to do that I really enjoy. For this, I thank you very much. (Designer from Tennessee)

ENRICHED BY SPIRITUAL GROWTH

To Our Dearest Friends Joan and Andy:

Where do we start in telling you what you and Premier have meant to us? Not only have you given us an opportunity to grow a profitable business and push our God-given talents to their limits, but, most importantly, you have guided us spiritually. Beyond a shadow of a doubt, the best thing that has come of our years with you and Premier has been our faith in God. (Jewelers from Georgia)

Dear Joan and Andy,

Our family has benefited in so many ways from our involvement in Premier. We've certainly benefited monetarily, but more than that, we have grown in our relationship with the Lord, and that is a direct result of being associated with the Premier Family. Thank you. (Jewelers from Mississippi)

AN UNEXPECTED BLESSING: MARRIAGES ENRICHED AND FAMILIES STRENGTHENED

One of the joys of Premier for Joan and me has been to see so many couples doing this business together and seeing many families strengthened. Some husbands do Home Shows while others support their wives by caring for the children. It has become a joint venture for many couples. We didn't plan it that way. I wouldn't have known how to do it. It is something the Lord has done—a totally unexpected blessing.

Dear Joan and Andy,

Premier came into our lives before our marriage did. In fact, our entire married life is a direct result of Premier. My wife was selling Premier jewelry to put herself through college. She sponsored me into Premier so I could pay off some debt so I could marry her. We thought I would be an engineer and she would be a dietitian and that Premier would just last through college. Little did we know!

We attended a meeting in Memphis that changed our life direction. You spoke, but you did not talk hype or money. You talked about serving people and making a difference in America. We knew that this was what we wanted to do—and that we wanted to do it together. Our

236

lives will never be the same. We are working together in a business we love, impacting lives and making a difference. Because of your vision, we are living our dream. (Five Diamond Designers from Texas)

Dear Joan and Andy,

It is difficult to put into words what Premier has meant to us. The Lord has used Premier to provide for our family, to draw us closer together, and to allow us more time to raise our own children. It has given us opportunities to minister to our Hostesses and to our Premier Family, and has given us the best friends we have ever had! Thanks, Joan and Andy! (Six Diamond Designers from Kentucky)

ENRICHING THE LIVES OF OTHERS

Dear Joan and Andy,

We are so excited to be associated with Premier. We are grateful to you for proving to the business community that a company can be successful that honors God and loves and serves people. We are so grateful for the lives you have touched and for the opportunity Premier has given us to be involved in loving and serving others. And to think that we joined Premier just to add a little money to our retirement checks! (Two Diamond Designers from Texas)

Dear Joan and Andy,

Premier came to us one year before I got laid off. Little did we know how much we would need Premier financially and spiritually that next year. I have seen my wife's confidence grow, and our love for each other grows stronger each year. Premier has been a constant source of strength and inspiration to us. We look forward to our years ahead with Premier. To be involved in a business with Premier's Philosophy and Purpose, that offers us an opportunity to impact so many lives, is truly a miracle. (Jewelers from Texas)

Dear Joan and Andy,

Premier is a miracle company that has truly honored God and served thousands of people. We would never have thought, or imagined, that such a company could exist in secular America. Premier may be the only business in America that provides an opportunity for spiritual growth and encourages ministering to others above money. Outside our church ministry, we are more excited about Premier than anything we have ever been involved in. (Jewelers from Louisiana)

Dear Joan and Andy,

We feel very blessed to be a part of Premier. Every day our Premier business brings us opportunities to serve and minister to others. Premier has allowed us to leave the stressful, demanding corporate world and have time to give to our children and grandchildren, as well as time to be with each other. The personal growth and rewards we receive through Premier continue to amaze us. Working with the people we sponsor and seeing them grow and meet their needs through their Premier businesses is a joy that enriches our lives. (Five Diamond Designers from North Carolina)

2009 Verse of the Year

*"A happy heart makes the face cheerful,
but heartache crushes the spirit."*

Proverbs 15:13, NIV

2010 Verse of the Year

*"Not to us, O Lord, but to you goes
all the glory for your unfailing
love and faithfulness."*

Psalm 115:1 NLT

CHAPTER TWENTY-THREE

Dreams Fulfilled

Our first reason for starting Premier Designs was, and still is, to get moms back into the home with their children, while still contributing to the family income. Secondly, it is to reassure single moms that there is life after divorce or widowhood, and to help them meet all their needs, including finances. Another reason is to help those like schoolteachers and Christian staff workers earn extra income to help with their family's financial needs. They impact the youth of America, and they are often underpaid and need extra income. Here are excerpts from some of the many letters we've received, showing how God has worked to fulfill Premier's Reasons for Existence.

MOMS GET TO STAY HOME

Dear Andy and Joan,

It is just amazing how the Lord continues to bless. Our boys have become so excited about Premier and the opportunity it has provided for their mom to be at home with them every day. Premier is such an integral part of our lives and family that we just want to say thank you for your vision for Premier and your steadfastness in seeing it through. (Three Diamond Designers from Texas)

Dear Andy and Joan,

I am so thankful God put Premier in my life. I was recently offered the full-time position of fashion coordinator for a clothing store chain. I had previously enjoyed this line of work and have several years of experience. If I took the job, it would mean that my three-year-old and nine-month-old would have to start going to daycare, but even so it was appealing. But after the Premier Rally, I knew what my decision would be, and I knew I was doing the right thing. I can do Home Shows four to eight nights a month for my business and make the same money I could working twenty or more days each month for someone else's business—and I can be home with our children. Premier has so much to offer and it sure came through for me. Thank you. (Four Diamond Designer from Georgia)

Dear Andy and Joan,

I was working in corporate America at a very large insurance brokerage, feeling very sad, beaten down, unappreciated and, most of all, feeling horrible that I had to leave my two beautiful children (ages 18 months and five years) in daycare. Then God opened a window in the form of a layoff. I lost my job. I was shocked and spiraled into a great depression. A friend of mine nudged me about Premier, saying I could get a low-stress, full-time job and do Premier to make up the income difference. I looked at what Premier had to offer and signed up that day. I already had some of the jewelry and I loved it, so now it was just a matter of booking those Home Shows! My career with Premier took off slowly but I was consistent. We prayed about going full-time and decided that I should be given a shot at it. I took my little guy out of daycare, and wouldn't you know it, my business exploded!

I cannot tell you how grateful I am for a wonderful, faith-based company like Premier. Thank you for reminding all of us that God didn't make a nobody. Thank you for providing me with an awesome way to care for my family's finances AND be a great mommy! (Builder from Florida)

SINGLE MOMS CAN SUPPORT THEIR KIDS

Dear Andy and Joan,

A little over twelve years ago, I joined Premier. Recently married, I saw Premier as an opportunity to help buy the extras we couldn't afford. At that time, we worked with college students at a small Christian school. Later I realized the long-term potential and options I would have if I continued to build my business. My heart's desire was not to put my child in daycare when I had a child. After ten years of marriage, Premier had become our full-time income and my daughter was born. Little did I know that three years later I would become a single mom. I know God has used Premier to provide for us financially. In addition, Premier has been a source of friendships, support, growth, and hope that I can share with others. Thank you for letting me be a part of the dream! (Seven Diamond Designer from Tennessee)

Dear Andy and Joan,

Like most people, I got in this business to earn extra income. As a single parent and sole support of my four-year-old son, I had to do something since my secretarial salary just didn't cut it. Little did I know how much I would gain—an extended family, lifelong friends, a strengthening of faith and persistence, and learning to love and accept people even if they don't always do what they say they will! It is out of financial, emotional, and spiritual necessity that I continue this business. In the words of my now eleven-year-old son, "Our lives wouldn't be the same without Premier." (Jeweler from Texas)

Dear Andy and Joan,

A couple of years ago, when I was on the verge of finalizing a painful divorce after fourteen years of marriage, I was struggling financially as well as emotionally. Little did I know that through Premier my life would be changed forever. A prudent businessperson would gauge the benefits of Premier by the "bottom line"—and that has been well above my wildest expectations. But that is just the tip of the iceberg in terms of what Premier has done for me as a single mom. The biggest treasures to come from my association with Premier have been friendships, the reaffirmation of values, and hope—something I had not felt for a long time. Now, not only have I been able to reestablish myself, but I recently purchased a beautiful home in my own name! From the bottom of my heart, thank you, Andy and Joan, for taking the time to give your attention and love to those who need it most—single moms like me! (Two Diamond Designer from Ohio)

HELPS THOSE IN FULL-TIME MINISTRY

Dear Andy and Joan,

My Premier story started in a very tragic way four years ago when our fifteen-year-old daughter ran away from home. Up to that point, I had had a perfect, story-book life. All of a sudden, my daughter was gone and I didn't know where she was. My marriage began falling apart. My husband is the pastor of a large church, and because our marriage was troubled, things at the church began to go wrong. In just a few short weeks, my wonderful, storybook life was totally wrecked. I became depressed, even suicidal.

About seven or eight months later, I was introduced to Premier and signed a contract, without ever having been to a Home Show. I had no idea what was in store for me!

God used Premier to help me with my emotional healing. My only identity up to that point had been to be the pastor's wife and the mother of four children. Premier opened up a whole new world to me. It gave me confidence and purpose. My daughters are now in college, and our Premier money is helping pay for that. My family has been put back together. My marriage has been restored. Our church is moving ahead once again. I thank God for Joan and Andy Horner and for Premier and what it has meant in my life. (Jeweler from Oklahoma)

Dear Mr. and Mrs Horner,

I wasn't excited about going to a jewelry show, but I wanted to help my mother-in-law. When I heard the opportunity Premier could offer me, my ears perked up. My husband wanted to start his own business to support us while he got into full-time ministry, but in the meantime, we needed some extra money. I had two small children at home (ages two and three), and Premier opened the door for me to be able to stay home, not pay for daycare, and earn great money. I fell in love with representing a company with Biblical principles! I look forward to being in Premier for many years! (Builder from Ohio)

Dear Andy and Joan,

At the time Premier was introduced to me, I was teaching first grade, assisting my husband in his church music ministry, and trying to meet the needs of our two daughters. We knew that our girls needed more of my time and attention, but there wasn't more time I could give them. We had financial needs beyond one salary; we were barely making it. We needed to make a change for our daughters' sakes.

Dear friends of ours invited us to dinner to share a business opportunity. I really didn't absorb the details, but I could see the genuine joy and excitement in their faces. It was obvious that this had affected their lives for good.

My husband immediately knew that this was for us. For the first time, he saw hope for our financial future. It sounded good, but I struggled about the commitment for months. I would tell our friend yes, and then fear and self-doubt would reign, and I would back out. Finally, school was ending, and I decided to step out in faith and trust God. I still remember driving to Home Shows and feeling so frightened that tears would run down my cheeks. God enabled me to do what seemed impossible.

I have always loved my husband's music ministry, and I have always cherished being his wife, but at times my identity seemed lost as an individual. God used Premier in my life to help me understand that I was special to Him as a person. He has given me a personal ministry to ladies outside of our church that I could never touch any other way.

We look at our lives and cannot imagine life without Premier. We have grown personally, spiritually, and financially. We thank God for you both and for Premier. It is so much more than just a jewelry company. (Four Diamond Designers from Texas.)

SUPPORTS MISSIONS AROUND THE WORLD

Joan and I have always been involved in missions in America and other countries. It was because of our desire to support ministries that we were motivated to launch Premier. Our prayer was that the company would be used to provide security and income to all who joined us and that there would be overflow to send to ministries at home and abroad.

Supporting missions is not something that we market or use to persuade people to join Premier. It is a private endeavor that we are privileged to be a part of. Here are excerpts from a few of the many letters we receive each month letting us know how God is working around the world.

Dear Premier Family,

Our hearts are full of joy for what the Lord has done during this summer at our camps. We had 400 campers. Thirty-one came to know the Lord as Savior, and 236 dedicated their lives to serve Him. Thank you so much for your continued help in prayer and in support. (Mario and Norma Portillo, Word of Life, Perugia, Italy)

Dear Friends,

I want to take this opportunity to express our deepest gratitude to you for your continued monthly support and donating Christmas presents to the children of the Matamoros Children's Home. Please continue lifting us up in your daily prayers. (Dr. Saul and Maria Camacho, Children's Home, Matamoros, Mexico)

Dear Andy and Joan,

I just want you to know how grateful I am from the depths of my heart for your consistent service to me and to our ministry. Thank you for your generous gifts to CitiVision, Transformation Life Center, the Love Kitchen, and the Manhattan Bible Church. Thousands of people are being blessed and are encouraged daily because of your generosity. Thank you. (Tom and Vicky Mahairas, CitiVision, New York City, New York)

Dear Premier Friends,

We are grateful for your good letter and want to thank you for the encouragement it is for us to know that you are upholding us in prayer. It is really wonderful to see all the exciting things that God is doing through Ireland Outreach. We thank you for being partners with us in this ministry. We are truly humbled and continue to praise the Lord for the privilege of being His servants. (Jim and Jean Gillette, Ireland Outreach, Dublin, Ireland)

Dear Friends at Premier,

I would like to express my appreciation for your gift. Thank you for participating in our ministry in this way. Many things are happening here in Poland. During the first four weeks of our camping season, 315 people made salvation decisions and 160 made dedication decisions! We thank God and thank you for your interest in our ministry. Thank you for your desire to pray for us. Your prayers mean very much to us. (Maly and Ewa Dwulat, Proem Ministries, Warsaw, Poland)

Dear Friends,

Greetings to you from rainy Uganda. A lot has been happening and we thank the Lord for open doors. During the last three months, we have seen over 1500 trusting Christ as their Savior. We have had 22 leadership training sessions in local churches, and over 200 schools have been put under our care by the Church of Uganda. The Gospel is being shared. These are great opportunities, and we thank the Lord. (Thomas and Faith Obunde, Word of Life, Kampala, Uganda)

Dear Premier,

In the last few weeks we have ministered to hundreds of families affected by disability at our JAF Family Retreats, plus we have delivered just short of 1,000 wheelchairs and Bibles thus far this season. Hearts are opening to the good news of Jesus Christ, depression is lifting, marriages are being mended, and families are being united. Thank you for your prayers and your gifts. (Joni Eareckson Tada, Joni and Friends International Ministries, California)

Conclusion

’m Michael. Remember me from the beginning of the book? I’m Linda’s husband who promised to share with you why Premier has changed our lives. I’m sitting here in this gigantic Convention Center surrounded by thousands of women and a lot of their husbands. As Andy’s "Lest We Forget" speech charges toward its conclusion, I’m thinking, *Why are there tears on my cheeks?*

I’m a baby boomer. I’ve lived through the Forrest Gump years and they were not a box of chocolates. For me, life’s been more like a box of firecrackers that keep blowing up in my face. I saw my teammates go from sweating it out at a high school football game on a Friday night to being blown apart by booby traps in the steamy jungles of Viet Nam. But soon, the Peter, Paul and Mary flower children, who sang about love and caring for one another, took off their torn jeans and cut their braids. Then, decked in their new Armani suits and at the wheels of their Mercedes, they pushed to take over Wall Street, pushing after the almighty dollar just like their parents of the fifties.

The 1960s, '70s and '80s infected my heart with a hopeless, cynical despair. My slogans became: "Everyone's got an angle," "Don't trust a soul over thirty," and "You can't believe in anyone or anything!" The image of Andy Horner, this Irish kid turned American, flashes before me on the big screen. I can also look to the front of this auditorium and see the real man, humbly sitting on a stool sharing his heart—the wisdom of decades of life experience.

Maybe my cheeks are wet with tears because "The Star-Spangled Banner" really does mean something. There actually were flesh-and-blood Americans who believed enough in freedom, free enterprise and the right of the individual to pursue life, liberty and happiness to shed their blood. Maybe there is something to letting others know that you love and appreciate them. What else could cause women to light up like the sun when they are applauded and recognized for their faithfulness, not just their sales, before thousands of their peers? Maybe words like honesty, integrity, faith, responsibility and caring still do have meaning and provide a true foundation that makes even a simple transaction, like purchasing some jewelry, more than just dollars and cents?

And all this talk about God, Jesus Christ and the Bible—perhaps it's time for me to stop reacting to the way my parents crammed religion down my throat, and stop using the worn-out, college sophomore rebuttal against faith: "Look at all the hypocrisy in the lives of those who profess it." After all, if this whole spiritual thing is bogus, why do I get so angry at a TV evangelist who is immoral? Maybe it's because deep inside, I do know what the real Jesus Christ stands for and who He actually is. I'm thinking I might sit down with Andy, or one of the other Leaders of Premier, and have a talk about their personal Jesus thing.

Premier isn't for everyone. Most people aren't going to travel around their town or city doing Home Shows. If they did, who could be invited to buy the jewelry? But everyone needs to take a long, thoughtful look at the values that Premier stands for. I just caught Andy Horner saying something about purpose. He usually gets the last word in Premier, so it's only fitting to listen in as he drives home his message:

> The Purpose of Premier, *our* Purpose, is to enrich every life we touch. We believe in a God who is able to help us to do this. Our Plan is to go into the homes of America and bring hope where there is often divorce, despair and meaninglessness. We want to help people smile again. Does this mean everyone is going to love you? Does this mean you will all be tremendously successful? Does this mean it will be easy? No!
>
> When I was in the heart unit at Baylor Hospital a few years ago, God was good to me. He gave me a warning signal before I self-destructed. I remember lying there in surgery looking at the video of my heart as the doctors

maneuvered their scope and their "roto rooter" to clean out my arteries. While they worked on my heart, I said to the doctor, "Where are the batteries for that thing?" He said, "What thing?" "My heart. What keeps it beating? Where do you have it plugged in?" He laughed and kept probing. "I guess it's just a little luck," he said. "No way!" I said. "It's not by chance. It's an answer to prayer. Don't you realize you have an army of my family and friends praying for your skillful hands right now, many of them right out there in the hallway?"

The cardiologist finished his delicate vascular plumbing job, and they rolled me into intensive care. Lying in the bed next to mine was a man whose stomach was all cut up from a fight the night before. Across from me was a lady who was not expected to live. I couldn't move, but then a quiet peace came over me. Never in my life have I had such a peace! Never so much joy! Folks, when I came out of that hospital, I came out with a message— a message I'm going to proclaim regardless of what anyone says.

I believe there is a God who created us in His image. Made "in the image of God" means that every one of you is priceless and needs to be treated with tenderness and respect.

I believe in my mom's tattered old Bible and the Biblical principles she taught me from the beginning way back in Belfast. I spent years rebelling against the Bible, then years defending it; now, I just let it speak for itself. It can fight for itself. It will endure.

I believe in the Bible's message—the power of Jesus Christ to give us forgiveness and eternal life. His personal presence in my life is my hope and joy.

I believe in the power of practicing the truth, not just preaching it. There have been enough high-sounding sermons. What people need to see are the actions. At Premier, we want to live what we say. We need the actions of commitment to home, to church and to our country. The home should be more than a place of wood, bricks and furniture. It should be a place where a family can find love, true values and acceptance. Without my faithful, skilled wife at my side, there would be no Premier. There would be no fulfillment of our dreams. She's not just my lover. She's my best friend.

Is Premier a Christian company? No! There's no such thing as a "saved company." Jesus died and rose again for individuals, not for corporations. Do you have to be a Christian to become a part of our company? Absolutely not! We are going to love and accept you, right where you are, and whatever you believe. I do believe in the Bible and in Jesus Christ. I believe in Him because I have actually seen His power change my life, and Joan's life, and thousands of others. But every individual has to decide for himself or herself.

Does this commitment to honoring God mean that we don't do our homework when it comes to business procedures and accounting practices? Look at the books and our operating procedures for yourself. You've seen the graphs and tables of our solid, controlled growth. The label "Christian" never becomes an excuse for sloppy business in this company.

It's the American Dream—to arrive in North America as an immigrant, the son of an alcoholic father and a scrub lady, and to rise to the top of a multimillion-dollar company. I've lived this dream, but the real riches come only when you learn to focus your life on enriching others. It's when you start giving yourself away that your real bank account begins to swell. Premier's bank account is full. We are financially strong. But the true wealth is sitting right here before me. It's *you*, and all those who have united with us to honor God and to enrich every life we touch, as we bring a dose of hope into homes across America. All this didn't happen just by chance. The Ultimate Designer brought this about, and He will see it to the end.

Have You Stopped to Smell the Roses?

*I*t is great to be involved in a company that is successful. It is even better when you know that many lives have been enriched as a result. But on the journey we can get extremely busy. Time with family and friends can begin to erode. Our priorities can get out of order and our lives out of balance. Instead of putting God first, family second and business last, our work creeps into first place, and family and God get whatever time is left. If our priorities stay out of whack, we will experience stress and broken relationships that can destroy us and drain all the joy from our lives. This can happen even when we are doing good things, and we can be trapped before we even realize what is happening.

It happened to me. I was very much in love with my work. Then one day, I was in Florida sitting by the window, looking out at God's creation—the beautiful sky, billowing white clouds, the azure blue ocean and roaring surf on the beach. I looked with wonder at all the beauty. I was tired physically and mentally, and my mind was muddled. I prayed and I sat. Then I took out a pad of paper and a pencil and wrote: "Have you

stopped to smell the roses God has given you today?"
A little poem emerged as I sat there.

I thought about all the blessings God had given
me, and I stopped to actually thank Him! It felt so
good. My mind cleared. I decided to do this as often as
I could—stop for just a moment and thank God for all
He has done for me, this day. This time became for me
"the pause that refreshes." It is the antidote for over-
working and a way to keep my priorities in balance.

In His Word, God tells us, "In everything give
thanks" (1 Thessalonians 5:18, NIV). You cannot be
thankful and unhappy at the same time. For me, the
story of Premier Designs is so amazing. I thank God
for what He has done for Joan and me. He can do the
same for you.

HAVE YOU STOPPED TO SMELL THE ROSES GOD HAS GIVEN YOU TODAY?

Have you ever stopped to smell the roses God
  has given you?
A world created so beautiful with a sky so blue.
The sun to warm us throughout the day.
There's the moon at night to light our way.
A breeze to cool and softly say . . .
*"Have you stopped to smell the roses God has
  given you today?"*

We work so hard and that's not bad.
And there are days when sometimes we're sad.
We are so occupied and concerned with what is
  going on,

That we fail to remember the real values our
    lives are built upon.
My family, friends, being loving and caring will
    always be
The things in life that matter most to me.
It just seems that no matter how I try along my
    way,
I fail to stop and *smell the roses God has given
    me today.*

It's not too late for me to decide
That from now on I can abide
In knowing what God has done for me.
He has blessed me with such a wonderful wife
    and family.
And that's not all—because of God's grace and
    love for me,
He's given me hope and a home in heaven some
    day to be.
I thank Him daily for loving me and for His
    grace that set me free.

Another day He has given me,
A beautiful sunrise for me to see.
No matter how busy I may be,
I must remember to keep in mind along my way
To stop and smell the roses God has given me today.

APPENDIX

Time Line

1924   Born in Belfast, Ireland.

1931   My mother decides to emigrate to America, leaving Belfast, Charleville Street, friends, and the land she loved. Due to health reasons, we are redirected to Woodstock, Ontario, Canada.

1932   Plan to attend the Brethren Assembly, but are not received because of no letter of commendation. End up at Oxford Street Baptist Church.

1934   School district lines change. Live on north side of street and transfer to Princess School. In school with Joan Taylor all through high school.

1935   Accept Jesus Christ as my Savior at Oxford Street Baptist Church.

1940   Mother purchases a Ford car for me to drive her to the building we are cleaning at night. This car is my ticket into the Joan Taylor group—a step up for an "East Ender" in Woodstock.

1941   Join the Royal Canadian Navy at seventeen-and-a-half years of age to get away from home and serve my country. Joan acted as secretary to Lee Forbes, formerly of Austin, Texas.

1945   Home on leave and date Joan Taylor. Discharged in October, and I am much in love.

1946   Marry Joan March 9. This is unthinkable as we are from different economic and social-class backgrounds.

1949   Because of Joan's desire to live in America, we apply for our visas.

1950 Board a train and enter America through Buffalo. Head to Boston area to work for my brother. This does not work out, so we head for Austin, Texas. Eight weeks later, I find a temporary job. Go to work Monday morning. The place is empty as it is May 30—Memorial Day. We make a hasty decision to go to Dallas, Texas, where we know no one. We make contact with Bill and Mary Blair. Bill has a brother, Bert, in Woodstock who told us to look him up. Joan finds a job at Reserve Life. Works for a Christian supervisor, Marie Hunter.

1951 Invited to church by one of Joan's associates, Mrs. Ritchie. End up at First Baptist of Dallas. April 29, Joan accepts Jesus as her Savior, and I rededicate my life to God. One of the first people we meet is Mary Crowley. She is Joan's Sunday school teacher.

1952 At Texas Unemployment Commission, I overhear information about an opening for a supervisor at Johnson Wax. Land job despite no college degree.

1960 Promoted at Johnson Wax and relocate family to Racine, Wisconsin. Meet Don and Marion Placko, our apartment neighbors.

1961 The Plackos introduce us to Word of Life ministries.

1963 Return to Dallas and join Xerox Corporation.

1967 Accept a transfer and plan a move to California. Have a check in my spirit and remain in Dallas.

1968 Get reacquainted with Mary Crowley, who founded Home Interiors and Gifts. In July, I accept a position at Home Interiors.

1984 I leave Home Interiors and resolve never to get involved in direct sales again.

1985 In January we make our first trip to Argentina and Uruguay—our first exposure to international missions, which changes our lives forever. In February we receive a call from CPA and friend, Wendell Judd, which results in consulting with a direct sales jewelry company. Opportunity to get the company for practically nothing. I am excited, but my lawyer refuses to approve. In August, trip to Poland, behind the Iron Curtain, with Dave Wyrtzen. This gives me plenty of time to share my heart. Dave's counsel is to use my talents as an entrepreneur. Howard and Hazel Goddard stop by unexpectedly in October and encourage us to "go for it." Found Premier Designs on November 5 and establish the Philosophy, Purpose and Plan.

1990   Company splits when the president at the time starts his own business. Formation of Premier Prayer Partners.

1991   Premier purchases Haven of Hope.

1992   Creation of Horner-Premier Foundation.

1994   Premier enters into a partnership with Premier Manufacturing so we would have a local manufacturer.

1995   Premier Designs' tenth anniversary. Business retails over 60 million dollars, with 6,000 Leaders and Jewelers. Premier forms a partnership with Premier Communication Services, also known as PCS Production Company.

1996   Remodel Haven of Hope Training Center.

1998   Pay off Home Office building mortgage. Establish website. Joan Horner promoted to Executive Vice President.

1999   Break ground for addition to Premier Designs Home Office.

2000   Celebrate Premier Designs' fifteenth anniversary with a National Rally in the Dallas Convention Center. The Premier Family is joined by many of our Prayer Partners and missionaries from America and around the world.

2001   Move-in completed for newly constructed reception center at Home Office. Construction begins on new

Distribution and Warehouse Center at Home Office. Active Jeweler base tops 10,000.

2002   New Distribution and Warehouse Center opens at Home Office.

2003   Steady continued growth throughout the year. Natural gas discovered, lines drilled at Haven of Hope.

2004   Haven of Hope 16-bedroom Cedar Lodge completed.

2005   Celebrate Premier Designs' twentieth anniversary. Prayer Garden and benches, a gift from suppliers/vendors, installed at Haven of Hope.

2006   Greatest annual growth ever for Premier Designs with over $300 million in retail sales. Eighteen acres, including buildings, purchased for Haven of Hope, bringing total acreage to 100. New Fitness Center with gymnasium and track as well as a warehouse addition completed at Home Office. Joan's book, *Keeping It Personal*, is published.

2007   Organizational changes—Tim Horner is named President. Active Jeweler base hits 27,000, with 275 Home Office Associates. The online Replacement/Exchange was implemented.

2008   Distribution Services goes fully automated with a state-of-the-art picking and packing system.

2009   Andy and Joan Horner are inducted into the Direct Selling Association Hall of Fame. On November 25, Premier records the largest number of Home Shows in its history, with 10,262 Shows on a single day.

2010   Year-long celebration of Premier's twenty-fifth anniversary is highlighted at the 2010 National Rally held in Fort Worth, Texas, with over 9,300 Jewelers and guests in attendance. Andy and Joan are awarded honorary Doctor of Humanities Degrees from Dallas Baptist University. Active Jeweler base hits close to 40,000.